PRAISE FOR *HIRE YOURSELF*

"Now is the best time to become an entrepreneur and franchise owner-ship makes it easier. If you want to be your own boss and live life on your terms you must read, study, and follow the path laid out in HIRE YOURSELF. *It is clear Pete Gilfillan is on a mission to help people take control of their destiny through franchise business ownership."*

— AMIT Y. KLEINBERGER
Chief Executive Officer, Menchies

*"*HIRE YOURSELF *takes you by the hand and leads you from the initial stages of an idea about franchising to a successful investment and stellar startup. Pete provides real stories that you can relate to of others that have followed a similar path with practical resources to guide you through the entire process. A must read for anyone consider-ing franchise ownership!"*

— BORIS KATSNELSON
President, SpeedPro Imaging

"Pete Gilfillan makes a compelling case for exercising your option to HIRE YOURSELF. *With up-to-date facts and statistics, he reminds us of a new truth in industry: Loyalty isn't what it used to be! The days of the employer based career are fading, and in its wake is a new career model that allows smart, ambitious, talented, middle-aged ex-ecutives seeking a new path to control their own destiny through busi-ness/franchise ownership."*

— KURT LANDWEHR
Vice President, Franchise Development, Regis Corporation

"With its direct, engaging tone and 'these-are-the-real-facts' approach, HIRE YOURSELF *makes a compelling case for the benefits of franchising and being an entrepreneur. Pete Gilfillan provides a unique perspective about the business model that seems perfectly poised to expand in nearly every industry."*

– ROCCO FLORENTINO
President and CEO, Benetrends Financial

"For the right person who finds the right franchise concept, entrepreneurship is an amazing journey to success. In HIRE YOURSELF *Pete Gilfillan shows you the steps to find the right franchise opportunity that will transform your unique talents into entrepreneurial success; to make a better life for you and your family."*

– RICK CROSSLAND
Owner, A Player Advantage

"Pete Gilfillan has written a smart, savvy, eminently reliable step-by-step guide to choosing the right franchise for you. HIRE YOURSELF *is loaded with great advice from the first page to the last."*

– BOB MCQUILLAN
Vice President, Franchise Development,
Hand & Stone Massage and Facial Spa

"If you believe that owning your own franchised business is in your blood, first get a head start by reading HIRE YOURSELF. *It offers solid, real world advice on making the very best choice for your goals and lifestyle."*

– DOUG SCHADLE
CEO, Rhino 7 Franchising

"If you had opportunity to read only one book before investing in a franchise business, I would strongly recommend you read HIRE YOURSELF. *Pete Gilfillan takes you on an exciting journey to not only learn if franchise ownership is right for you but how best to finance and structure your venture for long-term success."*

– GEOFF SEIBER
CEO, FranFund, Inc.

"HIRE YOURSELF *is a fantastic resource for anyone who's feeling fed up or burned out with the corporate world. Pete Gilfillan makes a compelling case for taking one giant leap into entrepreneurship to cure what ails you.*"

– KIM DALY
Senior Consultant, FranChoice

"*I got my start in franchising as a client of the process that Pete uses to match people with the right franchise concept. Having gone through this process myself, I can tell you that he has covered everything you need to know in evaluating and succeeding in a franchise business. If you are ready to take control of your destiny,* HIRE YOURSELF *needs to be the next book you read!*"

– RANDY CROSS
President of the Franchisor,
Fish Window Cleaning and a franchise owner with Fish

"HIRE YOURSELF *gives newcomers and experienced entrepreneurs alike an astute and insightful look at each step in the process of franchise investment. The step-by-step process that Pete has outlined is like getting the expert CliffsNotes to the hard learned lessons of not just starting a franchise, but also what you need to know before beginning any business venture! I wish that a decade and a half ago someone would have handed me* HIRE YOURSELF *as I would have entered into the world of being an entrepreneur and franchisor with the knowledge base needed to be years ahead of where I started from.* HIRE YOURSELF *will be a must read for all of our new franchise locations and should be for anyone contemplating being their own boss.*"

– DAWNYEL SMINK
President, Canyon Lands Insurance/ CLI Select Agencies

"*The knowledge and insight Pete Gilfillan delivers can help transform anyone's hard work for someone else into a dream-come-true franchise of their own. With the know-how in* HIRE YOURSELF, *get ready to design your own destiny.*"

– P. ALLAN YOUNG JR.
CEO & Co-Founder, ShelfGenie Franchise Systems

"When we think of entrepreneurship, we tend to get caught up in a traditional path, starting a business from scratch. HIRE YOURSELF illustrates that exploring the world of franchise ownership may finally be the answer to the often asked question, 'How do I realize my dreams and goals of a successful career?' Be surprised as you learn the realities of controlling your own destiny with the best kept secret, franchise ownership."

      – NICKI ANDERSON
President/CEO, Naperville Area Chamber of Commerce

"Starting your own business can be intimidating and lonely. HIRE YOURSELF makes you feel like you've got a stand-up guy who knows the process inside and out in your corner, offering equal measures of reassurance and good advice. Before you consider your next business opportunity, you should read and learn from this excellent resource."

      – DON MARKS
Chief Executive Officer, POP-A-Lock and Temperature Pro

"HIRE YOURSELF offers a thoughtful and affirmative look at the potential of franchising for those who've had their fill of corporate politics, job insecurity, and an ever-dwindling appreciation of the corporate loyalty that was once a linchpin of the executive career. He makes a compelling case for entrepreneurship that most need, given the intense struggle which exists between a person's Dragon (F.E.A.R.) and the dream that started the prospective franchisee out on their adventure to begin with."

      – MARK A. TITCOMB, II
Sr. VP of Franchise Recruitment, CertaPro Painters

"Pete Gilfillan has 'walked this road'...And, this book leverages his experience to help others honestly assess their purpose for work and to make an informed choice that will best serve them and their family."

      – WES KIMES
Vice President, Executive Services,
Right Management Chicago, IL

HIRE
YOURSELF

HIRE
YOURSELF

CONTROL YOUR
own DESTINY through
FRANCHISE OWNERSHIP

PETE GILFILLAN

Foreword by **DARREN HARDY**
Publisher & Founding Editor of *SUCCESS* Magazine

WWW.HIREYOURSELFBOOK.COM

Published by Advantage, Charleston, South Carolina.
Member of Advantage Media Group.

ADVANTAGE is a registered trademark and the Advantage colophon is a
trademark of Advantage Media Group, Inc.

Printed in the United States of America.

ISBN: 978-1-59932-447-0
LCCN: 2014956739

Pete@HIREYOURSELFBOOK.COM | 855-904-7900 | HIREYOURSELFBOOK.COM

Advantage Media Group is proud to be a part of the Tree Neutral® program.
Tree Neutral offsets the number of trees consumed in the production and
printing of this book by taking proactive steps such as planting trees in direct
proportion to the number of trees used to print books. To learn more about
Tree Neutral, please visit www.treeneutral.com. To learn more about
Advantage's commitment to being a responsible steward of the environment,
please visit www.advantagefamily.com/green

Advantage Media Group is a publisher of business, self-improvement, and
professional development books and online learning. We help entrepreneurs,
business leaders, and professionals share their Stories, Passion, and Knowledge
to help others Learn & Grow. Do you have a manuscript or book idea that you
would like us to consider for publishing? Please visit advantagefamily.com or call
1.866.775.1696.

This book is dedicated to Shannon Gilfillan—
my amazing and wonderful wife,
who inspires me to make a difference in other's lives;
and to Alex, Sarah, Kate, and Lauren Gilfillan,
my awesome kids, who make me deeply proud
of the young man and women they are becoming.

FOREWORD

A Special Message from Darren Hardy

Understanding, inspiring, and empowering entrepreneurs are the big ideas that get me out of bed in the morning. They drive my commitments as a publisher, author, speaker, and mentor. The thrill of sitting down with a phenomenally successful entrepreneur and learning what makes that person tick; the ability to share those insights with men and women who are just starting out (or moving up) in business; the opportunity to put my lifetime of experience in business to good use as a reference for the next guy—those are the experiences that shape me, shape my magazine *SUCCESS*, and shape my books and speeches.

Pete Gilfillan and I share a deep-seated and genuine enthusiasm for championing the aspiring entrepreneur. We've both known, maybe all our lives, that being self-directed and self-employed has a magic to it. Deep down, I think we all know that magic is out there waiting for us to capture it.

Lately, at my every opportunity—starting with my new book *The Entrepreneur Roller Coaster* and extending to pretty much anyone who will listen—I like to talk about time. Specifically, about this time, right now, when the rules for going into business are changing dramatically every single day. We stand at a unique moment in business history, a moment when technology has made it possible for anyone to reach out and connect with the world, with the public, and with the customer, in ways that weren't even dreamed of a decade ago. Or even a year ago.

What does it mean for aspiring entrepreneurs and for the legions of corporate workers who've been dreaming of going into business for themselves? It means this is the moment to make that happen. Decades from now, those who made the most of this window of opportunity will be looking back fondly, remembering how they found the courage to take a chance and jump on that Entrepreneur Roller Coaster at just the right time.

So what's the first step a man or woman has to take to catch the coaster? In my experience, the first—and hardest—is overcoming the crippling fear of stepping into the unknown. The easiest way to get over that fear? Read. Ask questions. Acquire the knowledge that gives you confidence in the choices you're about to make. Learn what that entrepreneur coaster ride is all about so you can hop on—thrilled and terrified, yes, but ready for the ride of a lifetime.

In HIRE YOURSELF, Pete Gilfillan has authored a book that shares an insider's knowledge and experience in making smart, informed choices in franchise investment. Pete speaks directly to the intelligent, hard-working men and women who might benefit most from taking a chance right now. At a time when corporate America seems less and less appreciative of loyalty and long-term service, Pete encourages readers to bet on themselves, to leverage their hard-earned skills, savings, and work ethics to their best advantage. HIRE YOURSELF is a roadmap to the possibilities of thinking outside the traditional career box.

In the first pages of this book, Pete Gilfillan credits me with saying something that gave him a metaphorical push to tackle an issue that matters to him: the issue of middle-aged corporate execs who find themselves laid off, downsized, pushed into retirement or burnt out—and yet never consider the option of entrepreneurship. And Pete really did tackle his topic, rolling up his sleeves and digging in to research, write and publish his message of creating career independence through franchise investment. I'm honored to have played a small part in encouraging him to bring this book to life.

In *The Compound Effect*, I wrote, "You make your choices, and then your choices make you." It's a quote that often comes back to me, from readers who've taken it to heart and made a life change, big or small. And it's a quote that Pete Gilfillan exemplifies to its best advantage. He chose the less-travelled path of entrepreneurship. He chose to take a chance to better life for his family. He chose to work tirelessly to make a success of his business. And he chose to build a whole new career centered around helping others like him find their way to entrepreneurial success. Pete made his choices, and then his choices made him. The result is an enthusiastic, ethical, self-made man with an enthusiastic, ethical, and truly valuable book to share.

If you're looking for a guide that explains not just the fundamentals of franchising, but the ins and outs of choosing and investing in one with a stellar concept, a reliable business system, and a commitment to successful franchisees, you'll find a wealth of information in HIRE YOURSELF. You'll find dependable facts, unique perspectives, and valuable insights into the potential of proven systems. You'll find a wealth of what-to-do and what-NOT-to-do tips. And you'll find it all written in the refreshingly direct and positive voice Pete brings to everything he says and does.

Pete Gilfillan is living proof of the success that can be achieved when you HIRE YOURSELF.

TABLE OF CONTENTS

FOREWORD – 13

A Special Message from Darren Hardy

INTRODUCTION – 19

PART I: WHO BETTER TO HIRE YOU—THAN YOU?

CHAPTER 1 – 23

The Changing Shape of Career Success

CHAPTER 2 – 47

Do You Have What It Takes to Succeed as a Franchisee?

CHAPTER 3 – 63

3,000 Concepts and Counting: How Franchising Works

PART II: FINDING YOUR IDEAL FRANCHISE INVESTMENT

CHAPTER 4 – 83

Know What You Want: Goals and Strengths

CHAPTER 5 – 99

Meeting Your Match: The Right Concept and Business Systems

CHAPTER 6 – 115

Finding "The One": Investigating the Top Franchise Concepts for You

PART III: REAL STEPS TOWARD REAL SUCCESS

CHAPTER 7 – 139
Can You Afford It? Capitalizing Your Investment

CHAPTER 8 – 161
Four Foundations of Franchise Success

EPILOGUE – 181
Are You Ready To Hire Yourself?

ACKNOWLEDGMENTS – 183

ABOUT THE AUTHOR – 185

INTRODUCTION

This book is for all the successful, hardworking people who know in their hearts they could make it on their own. For those of you who have that nagging sense there could be more to your working lives, more to *you*, than just putting in hours and waiting for retirement. For those who have been displaced from promising careers and are struggling to find the right path back to positive productivity and substantial earnings. Each of you has had the inkling—or even outright conviction—that you could be more successful, more fulfilled, more satisfied if you could invest in yourself.

The paths that led us here are many, but our dreams and goals are the same—to parlay our experience and past successes into a brighter future. We want to leverage our talents and treasures into something we can own—in an investment in our futures.

Perhaps you've been downsized in the sluggish economy. Perhaps you opted for an early buy-out or retirement to investigate your career options. Maybe you're tired of toiling long hours for a career that's unfulfilling and exhausting—investing in a company's success, but personally treading water. Or maybe your own career is good, but you're looking ahead to a job market where your children won't have the same kind of opportunities you did—and you want to build a family business where multiple generations can contribute and thrive.

Why not invest in yourself?

This book is about becoming happier and wealthier by betting on your own talents, skills, and abilities—and about mitigating your risk and maximizing your rewards by investing in a proven business concept. This book is about hiring yourself to own and run a successful franchise.

Franchise ownership is rapidly expanding and touching almost every industry. In fact, there are over 3000 different franchise brands available today. Whether you're taking your clothes to a dry cleaner, getting new locks on your door, or having your windows cleaned, chances are good that a franchisee will be doing the work. These franchisees didn't have to reinvent the wheel, or spend money and time developing systems and proving the viability of their ideas. They simply took advantage of opportunities in this growing area where they could decide what they wanted to produce, invest in a business, work hard, and bet on themselves.

No doubt, you've picked up this book for a reason. Are you ready to take the first step toward following your dream? Do you want to escape working for someone else, or to set up a plan to diversify your business portfolio before the next economic downturn? Maybe you've always wanted to be an entrepreneur, but don't know how to get started. Whichever scenario fits your situation, this book is for you.

Renowned management scholar Peter Drucker once said, "The best way to predict the future is to create it." I hope this book will give you the courage to choose your own future and take control of your career through successful franchise ownership.

PART I

WHO BETTER TO HIRE YOU— THAN YOU?

CHAPTER 1

THE CHANGING SHAPE OF CAREER SUCCESS

*"When we are no longer able to change a situation,
we are challenged to change ourselves."*

—VIKTOR E. FRANKL

ow fitting that the man who is the driving force behind *SUCCESS* should be the one who helped put me on the path to my own personal mission, and to my desire to write this book. I heard *SUCCESS Magazine* publisher Darren Hardy speak at a conference a few years ago, and he made a statement that caught my ear and rattled around with me for days: *The size of your life is determined by the size of the problem you solve.*

After years of swinging too far in one direction or the other, I had reached a point of personal and professional balance in my life. I'd found a way to work for myself and take care of my family. I was ready for my next step at that conference—and the idea of solving a big problem, of taking on a meaningful challenge, came at just the right moment.

Here is the problem I see, the one I think I can help solve: An entire generation of my peers in the workforce is caught up in the mindset that traditional employment is the only career option available to them. Unfortunately, for reasons beyond our control, that career model is failing many of us. There are far too many valuable contributors who've been laid off, downgraded, derailed during career transition, prematurely retired, overworked, or undervalued. There is a viable alternative to the standard-issue job, one that helped changed the direction of my career—and ultimately of my life.

That alternative was investing in myself through franchise ownership. It was a choice that allowed me to take control of my life and my fate.

Darren Hardy tells me his goal is to help inspire and launch a *million* new entrepreneurs in the next 3 years. I hope to contribute to that monster of a goal by sharing the opportunities available through franchising--opportunities that have changed *my* life— with folks who, like me, have had enough of marking time in tired corporate jobs. If you crave a new direction and the independence that comes with building a business of your own, this is a path I can illuminate for you.

I think of the franchise option as *Entrepreneur Lite*. It creates a fast-track to business ownership, but it doesn't require a brilliant and original concept—or the development of systems, processes, and procedures from the ground up. In the franchising model, all that has already been done. Someone has already dreamed the big dream, figured out how to make it work, and marketed and sold their way into a well-defined niche. Now they're looking for an investor and partner to build on that success.

I know far too many hardworking people who get pushed out or burned out and then spend months or years and their life savings on job hunting—people who never give a minute's consideration to going out on their own. They're too intimidated by the unknowns and perceived risks. Many of those individuals have the right resources, skillsets, and experience to succeed in franchising.

> *In franchising, someone has already dreamed the big dream, figured out how to make it work, and marketed and sold their way into a well-defined niche. Now they're looking for an investor and partner in building on that success.*

Every year, I help hundreds of prospective business owners look at their options and consider the viability of investing in a franchise. Some do, some don't, some put the idea on the back burner for another day. My role as a franchise consultant is that of matchmaker—helping promising candidates and proven, successful franchisors find each other. I love being the person who brings a great candidate to the right opportunity. It's an amazing thing to be able to help the American Dream of business ownership on its way.

The problem I hope to solve is how to illuminate the franchise option for the people who have the most to gain from it—those who would thrive if they had the chance to hire themselves. If any of these scenarios describes your situation, that might be you—and you might have another worthwhile path to consider before making your next career move:

- Are you actively job hunting to replace a lost career position?

- Have you *been* job hunting for months or years, and are you starting to think about throwing in the towel rather than continuing to find only part-time, contract, or low-pay positions?

- Do you think the writing's on the wall at your corporate job, and you want to be ready if and when the pink slips come to your side of the building?

- Are you looking for a career change—maybe because you've taken an early retirement or finished a military career, or perhaps because you just need a new challenge?

- Are you grinding away at a job that's beginning to grind back, taking a toll on your health, on your family, and on your spirit?

- Do you want to increase your business portfolio by investing and diversifying via business concepts with proven records of success?

For some people, franchising comes along like a storm of opportunity, blustering in and offering a new, quick, and total change. But for most, it's an idea that lurks, that knocks, that begins to carry a little weight, and that eventually wants to be heard. It's an idea that, as it matures, offers a way to build a bridge out of corporate dependence and into entrepreneurship.

If you've ever wondered if owning a franchised business might be for you, then the chapters that follow will give you both overview and insight into the kinds of opportunities that are available, who stands to benefit most from pursuing them, and how to go about learning more and exploring your options.

A LITTLE ABOUT ME

In my work with franchisees, I'm often asked how I got into this business myself. To be honest, it took me a couple tries to make the leap. Like so many other good candidates, I had to be pushed to my limit before I was ready to take a chance on myself. I spent twenty years working for major corporations—fulfilling, demanding jobs that helped make me a strong businessperson. As much as I gained, though, those jobs took a big toll on the things that matter to me. In the end, you might say it took three strikes, each of them directly involving my family, for me to make a change.

Strike One, the first time I thought about taking my career outside the corporate safety net, occurred when my wife and I were living in Detroit, moving from a temporary apartment to a new house. Shannon was in the last months of a difficult pregnancy, on doctor's orders to stay in bed. I was working as many as fifteen hours a day, and on the morning we were scheduled to move, a crisis arose in my office. My boss forbade me to leave—and being a young, career-driven executive, I didn't. Despite her own better judgment and mine, my wife had to handle things herself. Not long after, she went into premature labor. On the cold, rainy Friday afternoon that I fought my way home against rush hour traffic to take her to the hospital, I was overwhelmed with worry and guilt. I hadn't been there when she needed me, and now she was in jeopardy. Our baby was born seventeen minutes after we arrived at the hospital.

I would have been crazy to not stop and wonder if the commitment my company required of me was too much.

Fast-forward several years, and Shannon and I were thrilled to have a fourth baby on the way in our growing family. We were living in Atlanta, and my company wanted us to relocate to California. Fair enough—we packed up and went and immediately started renovating a home. After just two months, though, I got new marching orders; my job was moving to Michigan.

Six months to the day after we'd arrived in California, we were moving into yet another home in yet another state. Our children were overwhelmed by being uprooted twice in quick succession; my wife was still pregnant with the same baby she'd been carrying in Atlanta. We had to ask our brand new neighbors to watch our young children when Shannon went into labor in the middle of the night—we hadn't even had time to find a babysitter. Strike Two.

During this time, I was working sixty to seventy hours a week, and often MIA as a father. My kids were growing up, and I was too busy to be there for their milestones. I was professionally successful, and I was grateful for my good job, but this was not the life I wanted.

I'd been raised in an entrepreneurial family, and so I often dreamed of owning my own business and finding a better balance. In 2006, when my company offered separation packages and laid off a large number of workers, I accepted a package and walked away.

After a few months of reconnecting and recharging at home, I was ready to take a risk, to invest in a business and work for myself. But the timing wasn't right—we had four young kids, and owning a business was not a dream my wife shared. She wanted—and who could blame her?—to put security first.

> *I was professionally successful, and grateful for my good job, but this was not the life I wanted for myself or for my family. I dreamed of being an entrepreneur and finding living life on my own terms.*

I took another corporate job, and climbed back onto the executive ladder. It was a solid position and provided a great income, but it required long hours and endless travel. I would wake up some mornings and have to stop and mentally retrace my itinerary—just to figure out what hotel, what city, or even what country I was in. I was gaining weight, always tired, and moving toward elevated blood pressure. Worst of all, I was distant from my family. I still remember a day when I was getting ready to go overseas, and my daughter was holding onto my leg, crying and begging me not to leave. You might as well have put a knife in my heart. It all added up to Strike Three.

It was time for a change. Shannon and I sat down to dinner one night and started talking about where our lives were going—how continuing on our current path would impact our marriage, our family, and my health. By the end of the evening, we had decided to reset the course of our lives. It was time to take control of our future. We would take a leap of faith, and I would take my chances as an entrepreneur.

We knew we were in for hard work and sacrifices. Making it as a franchise investor takes a huge commitment, just as does making it as a corporate employee. The distinction, for us, was about *who* would determine what was worth our time and energy.

A few months later, we leveraged our assets to buy multi-state rights for a junk-removal franchise, and I began a career not of cleaning out basements and garages, but of developing the territory, bringing in new franchisees, and building the brand. At the end of the first year, I was bringing in a solid cash flow, and I was also realizing that helping people make the leap to franchise ownership was the most satisfying part of the work. I loved making a good match, bringing the right people together, and seeing them make the life-changing decision to hire themselves. I knew this was the kind of career I wanted in my future.

I wanted to be a part of matching the right people with the right concepts. Several months after investing in my own franchise, I was given the opportunity to join a highly regarded group of franchising consultants—FranChoice—and I've been relishing the rewarding work of being a franchise consultant ever since.

My family life, my professional life, and my health have all improved since I took that first leap into franchising. It truly changed my life.

THE DECLINE OF THE COMPANY CAREER

The story of the first twenty years of my career is like that of thousands—tens of thousands—of middle-aged American executives. Once upon a time, if we got in on the ground floor of a good corporation, worked hard, and stayed loyal, ours careers were made. We could make a slow (or speedy) climb to our potential, and we could count on job security—and with a little luck, some semblance of professional fulfillment.

But that was then; the career model of the "company man" (or woman) is less and less the norm. In fact, according to the U.S. Bureau of Labor Statistics, today's workers, on average, change jobs every 4.4 years. Those job changes can be driven by opportunity, but in recent years many are driven by necessity or hardship.

So what's changed?

During the recession of 2008, companies had to rapidly reduce overhead in order to survive. With employees representing a large part of that overhead, good people were laid off, given severance packages, or offered buyouts. Hard economic times hurt nearly everyone, but the downturn took an exceedingly harsh toll on workers in their forties and fifties—many of them smart and experienced with long track records of professional success. Why was this age group so adversely affected? Many were in their jobs for the long haul, operating under a career standard of loyalty and longevity. They were caught unaware and ill prepared for change.

Unfortunately, as the dust settles and the economy turns around, it's become increasingly apparent that the career model we grew up with is gone. The purge of experienced and well-paid workers during the recession gave corporations an opportunity to hire a younger and less-expensive work force. At the same time, companies are learning to operate leaner, and so the good jobs that do exist carry larger workloads and more pressure to perform—resulting in stressed out and unsatisfied professionals.

In another sea change, more companies than ever are relying on contract and part-time workers to get things done. Contractors get to leverage their experience and business acumen to help a company, but there's no job security, no insurance or sick time, and sometimes less pay. The employment firm Littler Mendelson predicted that contingent workers would comprise half of all jobs added following the recession. Half!

That's an awful lot of contingent workers—undoubtedly more than were banking on working part-time and on contract during their peak career years.

THE EVIDENCE IS EVERYWHERE

Let's take a look at just how bad the economic changes of the past few years have been for middle-aged workers:

- According to a study by the Urban Institute, workers over 50 years old who lost their jobs during the recession were 20 percent less likely to become re-employed than those ages 24 to 34.

- The unemployment rate for job seekers aged 55 and older more than doubled from December 2007 to March 2012.

- From 2007 to 2009, median monthly earnings for workers 50 to 61 years old declined by 23 percent, more than double the decrease experienced by their younger cohorts.

Jobs by the Numbers

4.4

Years the average worker spends in a job

23 percent

Median monthly earnings drop for 50–61 year olds between 2007 and 2009

45

Average number of weeks for workers ages 45–54 to find a job in 2013, vs. 20 weeks for workers 16–24

80

Percentage of Americans unhappy in their jobs

- Once workers are unemployed for more than six months, it becomes increasingly hard to find a job. In fact, according to a study out of Northeastern

University, employers would rather hire an applicant with little experience than one who's been unemployed for an extended period of time.

- In recent years, many workers over the age of 62 simply left the workforce when they were unable to find employment, as evidenced by a surge in new Social Security claims in 2009.

- In 2010, a large-scale survey by Deloitte Shift Index found that 80 percent of Americans were dissatisfied with their current jobs.

- In an August 2013 *New York Times* feature article, journalist Michael Winerip wrote about a grocery executive who was laid off just before his 57th birthday. During the next ten months, the man applied for 400 positions, had only 10 interviews, and was unable to get a job. Winerip has featured anecdotal stories of dozens of other unemployed, middle-aged executives—stories that are overall deeply discouraging. Many of the people he profiled were at the top of their game when they were laid off or fired, with backgrounds of professional excellence. But in follow up, those executives, many of whom had once earned six-figure salaries, were trying to make ends meet with part-time work, like retail sales, office temp work, even dog-walking. They were burning through their savings and becoming increasingly alarmed about their prospects.

The upshot of all the studies and statistics is a labor market where the odds are increasingly stacked against the mature professional whose strong career comes to a roadblock.

In my work as a franchise consultant, I speak with many people in the midst of forced—or at least pressured—career transition. They are struggling to find new employment at the same level of responsibility and compensation. Many of them deplete their savings while they fruitlessly search for a job comparable to the one they had before—and that savings is one of the key factors that could have given them more options than just any replacement job. The thought process is, "I was the vice president of marketing. I want to be the vice president of marketing again for another company." All too often, the reality is that they spend a lot of time, energy, and capital trying to find something that isn't there anymore. The buffalo are gone. It's time to move on.

> *The upshot of all the studies and statistics is a labor market where the odds are increasingly stacked against the mature professional whose strong career comes to a roadblock.*

To move forward, it's necessary to keep an open mind, to lift up your eyes and look beyond the path you've been on all along. You're at a career crossroads. There *is hope,* but it lies not in plodding forward in the same direction as before, but In making a new and decisive turn. You can try to go back to the same kind of traditional job you've had in the past, maybe settling a little bit and accepting a lower income, or a lesser title. Even if you have the same responsibilities, you'll likely have to work harder because it's a leaner organization. The fact is, a paycheck doesn't guarantee stability, and it may leave you vulnerable. A company can choose if they need or want your services today, tomorrow, or ten years down the line. As a business owner, you'd be in control of your own future. Why not bet on yourself and leverage the skills you've developed into something new that is really yours?

AN ALTERNATIVE PATH: FRANCHISING

Somewhere between muddling along at the whim of the corporate world and diving fearlessly into an untested venture is where you find franchising—business ownership sheltered by proven products, methods, and programs. You don't need to be the next Richard Branson, nor do you need to build a business from scratch. Instead, you can invest in an established business model. Franchising is about working *for* yourself, but not *by* yourself.

What exactly is a franchise? In the franchise business model, companies (franchisors) sell the rights to operate a business to the franchisee. The franchisee gains access to the company's marketing, training, and operating models, along with permission to promote the brand, product, or service. That allows the business owner to build on the success of a proven system.

Franchising is an important engine for our economy, and it is adding lots of jobs—an expected 200,000 just in 2014. In the United States alone, franchises employ an estimated 8.5 million workers. As a *Forbes* feature noted in October 2013, "Franchising happens to be a business approach that is booming at a time the rest of the U.S. economy is treading water."

There's certainly a lot of money moving through franchise businesses of all kinds. According to the U.S. Census Bureau, one of every nine retail dollars spent goes to a franchise. In a recent trend that underlines both profit potential and favorable risk level, even private equity companies are investing in portfolios of franchise concepts.

> *Somewhere between muddling along at the whim of the corporate world and striking fearlessly out into an untested venture is where you find franchising.*

The big question is: Who is in a position to benefit from the opportunities franchises have to offer? If you have a background of professional leadership, good people skills, an understanding of basic business math, capital to invest, the desire to go out on your own, and personal drive, then that person might be you.

The candidates I work with represent a wide swath of American workers. The biggest thing they have in common is simply that they are ready for a change and willing to take a chance to make change happen. I've included a few profiles here to share a sense of their backgrounds and goals. Perhaps you can relate to their stories:

Candidate A, Laid Off

I just worked with a man who'd had a successful career with a Fortune 1000 company, a bright guy with a big family and a couple of kids in college. Candidate A's company downsized, leaving him without a job. He decided to work with me to investigate franchise concepts at the same time he was hunting for a replacement job. About six weeks into the process, he didn't want to look at corporate jobs anymore. He didn't want to do the same thing again. He wanted to pursue a franchise opportunities. This candidate had planned to eventually retire to warmer weather in the Southwest. He decided to invest in a technology-based security franchise in New Mexico, getting him there ahead of schedule.

Candidate B, Burned Out

Some of my candidates are employed and making good money, but are burned out and tired of corporate politics and the intense personal cost of keeping up with executive-level commitments. Many have lost their passion. Some are parents—dads and moms—who are aching to reconnect with family and just can't find the time or energy. I worked with a woman a few years back who was half of a power couple. Candidate B was incredibly successful in high-end sales in the medical industry. She and her husband had two young kids, but she was on the road all the time and missing out on the day-to-day joys and trials of parenting. Candidate B didn't want to stop working; her dream was simply to find a fulfilling career path that would allow her enough flexibility to spend some quality time with her family. Candidate B invested in multiple locations of a fitness franchise that allowed her to continue to use her sales savvy and outstanding people skills. Now, though, she has more time for family. She even picks her kids up at the bus stop.

Candidate C, Planning Ahead

I recently worked with a successful individual who owns a large mortgage business. Even though Candidate C is doing well, he worries about the future, because knows he's in a cyclical industry. The economy or the government can change things in a minute, and his business could decline quickly. He came to me because he wanted to invest in something different. He said, "I want it to be simple. I want to get it off the ground so that I have diversification, so that if one thing zigs, then something else may zag."

Even those who are already business owners are now looking at investing in franchising, because there is so much opportunity associated with it. Candidate C chose to invest in a health-based franchise concept, buying the rights to multiple locations in Illinois.

Candidate D, Not Ready to Stop Working

It's a sad fact that the economic woes of the past several years have forced vast numbers of workers into early—and often unwanted—retirement. One of my candidates was in his mid-fifties and still vigorously involved in a great career when, through no fault of his own, he was forced to leave his company. The expectation was that this executive would simply retire, but that's not what he had in mind. He told me, "I have the capacity to continue to give. I want to keep working." What's more, he was not in a financial position to retire—just like most workers in their fifties.

Candidate D's realization that he was ready not just to continue his career, but to seek out real career progression, put him on a new trajectory—to look at franchising as a serious alternative. In the end, he chose to invest in a salon suites concept and opened up a whole new career path.

Candidate E, Creating a Fresh Start

One group of potential candidates with a unique edge in franchising is military veterans. Since a military career often ends after twenty years of service, many candidates find themselves at a first retirement in their forties, and they're looking for a new career challenge. I helped Candidate E, a veteran looking for just the right franchise investment to help him settle into civilian life, to build on his background of proud service and personal discipline by hiring himself to own a franchise.

Franchising can be a uniquely welcoming opportunity for veterans, because many franchisors offer incentives and even discounts on their franchise fees for vets. Some even help veteran franchisees with financing.

WHERE TO BEGIN

Here's what I suggest to the candidates I work with in franchise investigation: If you're searching for a change or a new position, whatever it may be, consider investigating franchise concepts at the same time. Take a dual path of research and due diligence and give franchising equal consideration along with all your other options. That way, you lose no time, and miss no chances.

WHY USE A FRANCHISE CONSULTANT?

By now you may be wondering—what's in it for this guy? After having a positive experience in franchising myself, I was intrigued and inspired to become more involved in the process of matching other franchisee candidates with companies to invest in. For the past several years, I've worked as a franchise consultant doing just that. Every year, I help hundreds of prospective business owners assess the viability of franchise investment. No matter what the outcome of the search, I enjoy the process of helping each individual make an informed choice.

It doesn't cost a candidate anything to work with a franchise consultant. Much like a real estate agent, a consultant gets paid by the seller (the franchising company) when they make a good match and a new relationship is born. I do recommend working with a consultant, since someone who works with franchisors and franchisees day in and day out has a unique perspective on the kinds of investments and partnerships that work well—and on those that don't.

My own office welcomes interested candidates, but if you're screening consultants on your own, ask these three questions to give you an idea of who you're dealing with:

1. *Is there a charge for your help in finding a suitable franchise investment?*

   In most cases, the answer to this should be no. You can absolutely get a great franchise consultant without having to pay. Established, successful consultants receive a referral fee from the franchisor when they successfully place a candidate. They don't ask candidates for money.

2. *What is your professional background and experience with franchising?*

   There is no standard set of credentials for a franchise consultant, so the answers to this question can be wide ranging. Things to listen for include professional experience in a franchise business; experience successfully placing candidates; and a professional, ethical approach to the search process.

3. *How extensive is your role in the process as I search for a suitable franchise and invest?*

   A good consultant's role goes well beyond introducing you to a suitable franchising company. Your consultant should be willing and enthusiastic about going through the process with you, helping you understand and prepare for each step. Examples of outstanding consultant service include helping you prepare for validation calls with existing franchisees; helping you connect with qualified experts on capitalizing a business; and being available and responsive to your questions and concerns. Don't underestimate the value of the trust factor: you should feel comfortable and confident in your consultant throughout the process.

A good consultant will have a system in place for evaluating franchise companies, one that helps his or her candidates weed out companies that are disorganized, undercapitalized, or unsuccessful on other fronts. There are four main qualities I look for in a franchisor, and your consultant likely has a similar list:

1. **Proven Systems**. This is the backbone of a good franchise business. The business must be repeatable, with solid systems and procedures in place that leave no room for error.

2. **Strong Brand.** A franchise doesn't need to be a household name to have a strong brand, but it does need a positive and consistently presented public image. If it's a new, early adopter concept, it should be well on its way to having those traits.

3. **Solid Financials**. Any franchise company you're considering making a sizable investment in needs to be financially strong.

4. **Happy Franchisees**. The best indication of a solid franchise opportunity is happy and successful franchisees.

Is it possible to ascertain all of this information on your own? Absolutely. That said, though, an experienced franchise consultant spends a significant amount of time vetting franchises to uncover the best opportunities, and has already done much of the research you'd have to begin at square one.

SUCCESS STORY: DOWNSIZED AND BETTER OFF

Background: Jim had a thirty-year career in the metals distribution business, working with one company in roles of increasing responsibility. When a private equity group came in and took the company public, corporate strategy and structure dramatically changed, and Jim's position was eliminated.

Search Process: Jim started a traditional job search, looking for an executive management position. At the same time, he thought buying his own business. After twenty years of experience running operating units, he was confident he could do it. His initial reaction to the idea of franchising was negative, but it grew on him when a broker explained how many widely varied options are available in today's market. For Jim, the biggest draws of franchising were affordability, established support and training protocols, and some franchisees' impressive track records of success.

Decision: Jim invested in a large-format printing franchise in northern Illinois.

Result: Jim says the elimination of his old corporate position is the best thing that's ever happened to him. The biggest challenge he faced was building brand recognition in his area, and he accomplished that through networking, referrals from customers, and community involvement. While he misses the camaraderie of corporate life and his annual incentive checks, he loves the fact that his time is his own and his business allows flexibility. "When one of my sons was on the high school soccer team," he says, "I was able to make every game. I'm working as hard or harder than I did in my corporate career, but I enjoy the work and don't mind that."

Best Advice: You cannot underestimate the importance of the validation process. Go in with your eyes wide open, and really learning from the owners you talk to. Find out what critical factors are in terms of success, failure, or mediocrity in the business. Ask questions of other owners to tell you about their challenges and things they wished they had done differently.

CHAPTER SUMMARY

- The model of the one-company career is increasingly far from the norm of success. The economy, technology, and information age have all contributed to this change in the workforce, and it appears to be here to stay.

- Middle-aged and older workers have been edged out of career positions and are finding it increasingly hard to find equivalent replacement jobs.

- Your life savings only last for so long. You could try to wait a career crisis out and hopefully beat the odds, but you could also choose to leverage your skills and assets in a different, more proactive way.

- Franchising is a legitimate and sometimes-overlooked option for middle-aged workers and executives—and it's a component of the economy that is booming.

- As the adage tells us, change is inevitable. The key to survival is adaptability and flexibility. If you can embrace change and capitalize on new and less conventional opportunities, you may find yourself in a more fulfilling career than ever.

THE NEXT STEP:

Go to the **HIRE YOURSELF** *resource page to learn more and take action*

QUIZ:
The Changing Shape of Success: Is it time to Hire Yourself?

WORKSHEET:
Career Assessment: Where You Are, Where You Want to Be, and How to Start Closing the Gap

FAST FACTS:
Why Now is the Time to HIRE YOURSELF

Go To:
HIREYOURSELFBOOK.COM/Resources

CHAPTER 2

DO YOU HAVE WHAT IT TAKES TO SUCCEED AS A FRANCHISEE?

"Twenty years from now you will be more disappointed by the things you didn't do than the ones you did do, so throw off the bow lines, sail away from safe harbor, catch the trade winds in your sails, explore, dream and discover."

—MARK TWAIN

hen I was in the fourth grade, I had to sell fertilizer to help support my school's hockey team. My dad decided that I was going to sell more fertilizer than any other kid on the team. He rehearsed my sales pitch with me, then dropped me off at an enormous subdivision of maybe three hundred homes, and told me to knock on every single door and ask the resident to buy fertilizer to support the team. After he drove off, I looked down the first street at all those houses, all those closed doors, and I took a deep breath and started knocking.

What did I learn that afternoon? First, that I was capable of selling a heck of a lot of fertilizer with nothing more than my hockey uniform, a stack of flyers, and a little bit of boyish charm. Second, I could make something happen with my time and energy. That knowledge would stay with me from then on—including the day when I finally decided to go into business for myself.

In my own family, I coach my kids to be sales champs and go-getters in their own right. Why? Because I firmly believe that the successful businesspeople of the next generation are going to need entrepreneurial experience and instincts. I want my kids to feel confident they can make things happen, can rely on themselves, can contribute to any cause they deem worthwhile.

GETTING PAST FEAR

How many of us, even as successful and hard-working adults, are still unsure of our own instincts and abilities, afraid to open ourselves to something new, or to take a chance for something we believe in? The corporate world can be a wonderful, secure, rewarding place—but if it was all that for you, we probably wouldn't be here together on this page. We're here to consider whether maybe branching out into a business of your own is a viable, potentially fulfilling, and profitable option—whether you could benefit from hiring yourself.

In my experience with hundreds of potential franchisee candidates, I've encountered fear and anxiety in even the most qualified and knowledgeable individuals. I've felt it myself. We all do. But experiencing reasonable fear and letting it dictate your choices are two completely different things. If fear is keeping you from investigating franchising, follow these steps to let reason take over:

Find your *why*.

Why are you considering this in the first place? Is your motivation greater financial security? More time with your family? A more fulfilling career? Identify your *why*, and use it to combat your fears. Whatever your personal *why* is, it's the thing that will get you through the tough moments.

Do your homework.

Spend all the time you need researching the option you want to pursue. Understand the actual risks and potential benefits—facts are the best tool available to allay unreasonable fears.

Look ahead.

Five years from now, where do you want to be? What stands between you and that goal? I try to help candidates to acknowledge their big fears—and then to take those fears into account in the research and planning stages of investment. I help them think through worst-case scenarios and figure out how they can prepare for each. You can't anticipate every possible hiccup, but you can mentally work your way through most of them long before any damage occurs.

INCLUDING YOUR FAMILY

One of the biggest mistakes candidates considering franchise investment make is leaving their significant others out of the loop. A franchise consultant colleague once told me that when it comes to including a spouse in investment research, "You can either do this *with* your partner or *to* your partner."

I learned this lesson myself—the hard way. When my wife and I decided I'd leave the corporate world and invest in a business, I literally locked myself in a room for nearly a month. At the end of that time, I emerged, amped up with excitement, and announced, "I found the business!" As I poured out my enthusiasm and certainty that this was the right investment, my wife just looked at me and said, "I don't get it." In case you aren't familiar with how this translates in spouse-speak, it means, "We're not doing it."

At that moment, I realized my mistake: I was doing this huge change *to* her, not *with* her. Lesson learned; the next business I started to investigate, I included her in every step of the process, and it made all the difference. *We* shared a view of the business and the choice to invest in it.

The moral of my story—and those of other investors who've made the same mistake—is simple: Your family will probably have many of the same fears that you initially had about franchise investment. If they haven't been through the whole journey with you—if you've been working on the logistics in your own head for weeks or months or years—you need to take the time to help them catch up. Acknowledge those fears, then build your family's confidence by sharing your business plan and laying out your realistic expectations for year one, year two, and even year ten. Their daily lives will be impacted by the changes you're making, and they deserve to be involved in the decision-making process.

As you share the reasons the change you're making is important to you, why you want and need it, and how it will change your lives together, you'll allow your family to share and embrace both your vision and your plan to see it realized.

> *If your family hasn't been through the whole journey with you—if you've been working on logistics in your own head for weeks or months or years—take the time to help them catch up.*

DO YOU HAVE THE FIVE Cs?

Once you get past any anxieties about franchise investment, it's time to do an honest self-assessment about whether you're suited to business ownership. What do you need to succeed? I spent seventeen years working at the Ford Motor Company, and as part of our process there we evaluated potential dealer candidates using four Cs as a guideline: Capital, Capacity, Character, and Customer Satisfaction. A solid candidate could demonstrate all four. In my work as a franchise consultant, I've also found a fifth characteristic—Cooperation—to be key. I use these same measures to help interested candidates assess their strengths and weaknesses. To date, they've served as an outstanding predictor of success. How do you measure up?

Capital

This first qualifier is the one we all know about, the one that some people allow to loom over the idea of franchise ownership, keeping them from investigating the possibilities. You must have some amount of capital available to invest in a business. Most franchise companies require a minimum level of liquid capital. They know that businesses often fail because they are undercapitalized, and they want to be sure franchisees are set up for success.

A number of costs beyond the initial fee need to be considered when you're investing in a franchise. There will be legal fees, equipment and inventory to purchase, rent, and royalty fees, for example. Keep in mind, too, that there is a ramp-up period with any business. You need enough money to cover your expenses during this time when more money will be going out than what is coming in. Meanwhile, the ordinary expenses of life continue, and you still need to support your family. You will need working capital beyond the start-up costs to keep yourself afloat until you've passed the breakeven point, at which you will be able to start paying yourself.

Your available capital will to some extent dictate your choices in franchising. Candidates sometimes expect to borrow all or most of the required investment, but the system doesn't work that way. Financing is available, and we will explore those options in more depth in another chapter, but don't plan on relying on loans to meet the bulk of your investment requirement.

From a financial perspective, franchisors are really looking for two things as they evaluate you as a candidate. First, they want you to have a certain level of liquid capital—cash on hand or other assets you can quickly and easily turn into cash. Aside from money in the bank, examples could include an equity line of credit on your home, stocks and bonds, or even leveraging your retirement accounts. A good general guideline is that you'll need a minimum of $50,000 to $60,000 in liquid capital for a service-based business, and anywhere from $75,000 to $100,000 for a facility-based business.

The second financial criterion a franchise company will consider is your net worth. If you seek financing, you'll need to back it up with something. Net worth is determined by the value of your assets less your liabilities. For example, if you have assets of $750,000 and you have $400,000 in liabilities, then your net worth would be $350,000. You can find a worksheet to calculate your net worth in Chapter 7.

There are companies that specialize in helping entrepreneurs leverage their available capital and raise capital if needed. Many options are available to secure financing depending on your particular circumstances, and we'll explore those in detail later. No matter how you choose to finance your new business, though, the bottom line is that lacking the necessary capital to successfully launch a new business, franchise or otherwise, is a nonstarter.

Capacity

The second "C" is for capacity. Although you may not need specific industry expertise to invest in a franchise concept, you must have a certain level of business acumen. As a business owner, you must understand people and how to motivate, lead, and support employees. Experience in sales and operations management will also support your efforts. It takes strong leadership skills to build a business and develop a reliable staff, and savvy hiring skills will save you from costly mistakes.

When assessing your capacity to run a business, consider how your prior experience will inform your decisions. You can hire an accountant if you don't have a good understanding of financial statements, but you do need to know how to read a profit and loss statement. Business is a numbers game, and you want to have a clear understanding of how it works.

Drive and goal orientation are important components of capacity, too. You need to be able to put together a solid business plan and follow it. Are you goal-oriented? You should know where you are headed, have a clear path to that outcome, and be prepared to make adjustments along the way.

I recently worked with a candidate who, prior to working with me, had partnered with a friend and business associate to start a new business. Their lack of a well-defined business plan cost them a ton of capital and time. They got off to a fast start, but took too many wrong turns because they didn't have a plan. Although they brought in a fair amount of revenue in their first year, their errors wound up costing them their profits and capital—and ultimately their business.

Fortunately, the core skills and business acumen you've developed throughout your career will likely transfer well to franchise ownership.

Cooperation

A key component of franchise ownership is understanding that you don't bear all the responsibility for driving the direction of the business. Your franchisor will have a detailed plan for you to follow—and they need to know you will embrace that plan in a spirit of cooperation.

Franchisors have to feel confident that you will follow their procedures and systems to create a consistent product and service upon which they can build their brand. That's the strength of a franchise, and the best reason for choosing to invest in one in the first place—those proven systems are already in place. By the same token, if you're the "my way or the highway" type, franchising is not likely to work for you. Franchisors don't want franchisees going rogue on them and bucking the system. They need smart, savvy business people who can take their proven concept and build a successful business. They need cooperative partners, not mavericks.

> *Your franchisor will have a detailed plan for you to follow—and they need to know you will embrace that plan in a spirit of cooperation.*

Character

Having good character is critically important—and it's built over a lifetime and throughout a career. Franchisors expect the people with whom they partner to operate with honesty and integrity. As a franchisee, you will be representing the brand, and franchisors will take a close look at how well you will do that. As famed entrepreneur George Van Valkenburg once said, "Leadership is doing what is right when no one is watching." Do you have a history of being honest and ethical?

Franchise companies may do a background check on their candidates to make an assessment of this quality. Be prepared to explain anything questionable in your history, including your interactions on social media. More than ever these days, how we live our lives is open to public view. A candidate's track record is important here because that offers the easiest way to assess character.

Another key component of character is work ethic. Owning a business takes significant discipline and commitment. You will have to be able to make good decisions and do the right thing when confronted with tough choices. If you have a strong record of hard work and commitment, you're already a step ahead when you start a business.

Hand in hand with your work ethic is your passion for your work. If you are passionate about the business you're starting, you'll be driven to do things the right way and represent yourself, your business, and your franchisor well.

Customer Satisfaction

The last big "C" is customer satisfaction. Warren Buffett famously said, "It takes twenty years to build a reputation and five minutes to ruin it." Volumes have been written about customer satisfaction—because it is the key to success for all businesses. For instance, I always buy my dress shoes at Nordstrom. Why? Because I once returned a pair of unworn dress shoes (still in the box) that had been in my closet for seven years—and they took those shoes back without any questions. It took them a long time to find the SKU number, but the store accepted my return. That is amazing customer service, and it's the reason I am fiercely loyal to the store. I have the same kind of relationship with my local Ford dealer—Hennessy's Riverview Ford—because on a Saturday when I didn't have time to deal with a dead battery in my car, they sent a technician to my house and replaced it. They went over and above for me, and I won't forget it.

Think about your own shopping and service provider experiences and how those interactions have shaped your opinion of businesses. Everyday transactions can earn your repeat business—or ensure you won't be back.

Do you have the desire and passion to create a superior customer experience? Franchise companies need to ensure that you will take good care of customers. After all, you are representing their brand. The level of service you provide not only affects your business, but it also affects the entire company. One botched customer interaction can cause a ripple effect through the entire franchise system. Social media and online review boards can raise that ripple to a tidal wave. There was a time when an unhappy customer might tell a handful of friends about a negative experience. Now, instead of speaking to five, six, or more friends, a dissatisfied customer might post an experience online for three hundred or more "friends" to see and share. Next, he might take a few minutes to log into a review site and share that experience with thousands more potential customers.

The fact is, it costs a business exponentially more time and money to attract a new customer than it does to retain an existing one. You will not succeed if your business drives customers away with poor service. The bottom line is that no matter what kind of product or service you intend to provide, you need to embrace and enjoy the challenge of delivering outstanding customer service.

Quiz: Is Franchising for You?

If you can answer yes to any of the following questions, franchise ownership might be the path for you:

- Have you accumulated a war chest of business skills but don't know where to head next?
- Do colleagues look to you as a leader?
- Have you always dreamed of owning your own business but didn't know where to start?
- Are you driven to deliver superior customer service?
- Are you able to follow systems and processes? Are you teachable and coachable?
- Are you willing to take financial risks to reap rewards?
- Do you have enough liquid capital to make a significant investment in a business?
- Are you willing to invest in yourself?

DON'T MAKE THIS MISTAKE:
LETTING NEGATIVITY RULE

Fair warning: As you navigate the process of learning about this kind of investment, it will seem like everyone has a horror story they've heard about franchise ownership—and they'll all want to share those stories with you. Friends and family members truly believe they're helping when they reach out with cautionary tales, and I encourage you to listen and, where appropriate, learn. But don't let others influence your choices with their own fears and anxieties about owning a business. Do your own research, and create your own intelligently designed plan. Then thank any naysayers for their concern, and make your own informed decision.

SUCCESS STORY: CONVERTING A BUYOUT INTO A BUSINESS

Background: Greg worked for a large company in engineering for eighteen years. When Greg's company created a new branch in India, he was involved in every aspect of the business there. He embraced the challenge of organizing and driving the start-up, and he and his wife began to think about the prospect of owing a business of their own. A couple years later, Greg's company was going through hard times and offered him a buyout package. That package provided some financial cover and the push Greg and his wife needed to start researching business investments.

Search Process: Greg's original plan was not franchising at all, but to buy a small manufacturing company. When he and his wife started looking, though, they weren't finding the right kind of opportunity. They thought franchising only applied to fast food or hair salons, and neither was the kind of thing they wanted to do. A franchise consultant introduced them to a broader spectrum of options, and advised that they look at the bigger picture: Where did they want to work? How did they want to grow the business? What kinds of things did they want to do all day? The consultant helped them work through all those issues.

Decision: Greg invested in a locksmith franchise.

Result: "We've been open for business for two months now," Greg says, "and at this point I can't imagine ever going back. At this stage of our life, this is a much, much better choice for us." Greg and his wife are partners now, with him running the operations side of the business and her in charge of marketing and finance. They've found they make a great professional team.

Best Advice: Think about the things that are really important to you, whether it's your finances or the people you work with. Don't think so much about the exact details of what the activity is, but think about the things that make you feel content. Then go find something that fills those needs.

CHAPTER SUMMARY

- Use reason and research to combat the fear and anxiety that will inevitably color your decision about whether to invest in your own business.

- It's important to have the five C's covered to build a successful business. Every franchisor knows it, and the good ones will carefully evaluate each candidate to ensure he or she will represent the brand well and can make money following the franchisor's business model.

- If you think you have what it takes, dare to head in a new direction. Hire yourself and break the mold (and the hold) of traditional employment.

THE NEXT STEP:

Go to the **HIRE YOURSELF** *resource page to learn more and take action*

WORKSHEET:
Assessing your Five C's: Capital, Capacity, Cooperation, Character, Customer Satisfaction

QUIZ:
Is Franchising For You?

FAST FACTS:
Tips For Moving Past Anxiety and Fear

Go To:
HIREYOURSELFBOOK.COM/Resources

3,000 CONCEPTS AND COUNTING: HOW FRANCHISING WORKS

"The only limits are, as always, those of vision."

—JAMES BROUGHTON

There are more than three thousand franchise concepts in today's marketplace, and although most people still think first of "fast food" when they think "franchise," franchising extends to almost every industry. Think about a typical day in the life of an American adult. If you wake up in the morning and head to the gym, you've likely had your first franchise encounter there. If you stop for a coffee on the way to work, odds are you've visited your second. If you go out for lunch, go to the dry cleaner, take your kids to karate lessons or a tutoring center, get a massage, have your car's oil changed, or pick up takeout for dinner—you've been patronizing franchises all day.

Franchise businesses have become ubiquitous in our day-to-day lives, and people are creating new ways to successfully use the franchise model all the time. Why the steady expansion of the concept to new industries and working systems? First, because business creators seem increasingly aware of the franchising option when they work out the bugs of their big ideas. They know they can reach more markets and more people if they can find a way to successfully franchise. Second, because investors like you, and like me, want to work for ourselves, want to have ownership of our careers, but we also seek the security of opportunities that have already been proven profitable. After all, why would we take on any more risk than is necessary?

NEW AND GROWING TRENDS

As a franchise consultant, there's one question I hear more than any other. Potential candidates, colleagues, friends, and casual acquaintances ask, "What's the next big thing?" Here's the thing about the next big thing: Franchising is, by definition, about success based on proven business models—and the proof that makes them solid investments can only come with the test of time. Not every business concept—even if it's genius—lends itself to franchising. Some successes just can't be duplicated.

Yes, there are flourishing areas in franchising. Among them at this writing are businesses that help parents to entertain and educate their kids; businesses that cater to thriving, retiring baby boomers; and green businesses. And yes, seeing a new trend coming can offer a great opportunity to invest and do well. But with franchises available in nearly every industry, I advise the candidates I work with to consider what's important to them, what their skills are, and how they want to spend their working days— all *before* they get to the inevitable question of, "What's hot?"

WAVE-MAKING BUSINESS MODELS

While I faithfully advocate for proven business concepts, I'm always amazed at the tremendous ingenuity franchisors show in coming up with new ways to implement the franchise model and make it profitable. For example, look at the Massage Envy concept. This franchisor took a traditional small business and created a win/win model that provides value to everyone involved. Customers get discounted massage services by having memberships; franchisees get a reliably steady stream of income from membership dues. The concept created a whole new segment in franchising—one I think we'll be seeing more of in the future.

Another franchise that came into the marketplace as a maverick and changed the game is 1-800-GOT-JUNK. This business, designed by an eighteen-year-old Canadian entrepreneur, was another innovative win/win idea. By utilizing a junk service, customers get rid of clutter, landfills are spared as much as 60 percent of those cast-offs, and useful items end up in the hands of charitable organizations that can use them. The concept has been duplicated and tweaked many times over by other companies—because it's a great idea that works.

There's no way to know what game-changer will come along next and invent a new concept in franchising, but these businesses are great examples of the kind of innovation investors love to see: models with outstanding customer value, reliable investor profit, and that extra something—be it a benefit to the community, to the environment, or another angle altogether—that makes them unique and memorable.

FRANCHISE STRUCTURE BASICS

While franchise concepts can vary wildly, there are a few basic guidelines you can use to help categorize and analyze your options. At its core, a franchise is simply a *way* of doing business—a method that works for providing a service or delivering goods to a consumer.

Franchises generally fall into two categories, *facility-based* and *service-based*. Each has its own strengths and drawbacks, and one of the first decisions you'll have to consider when you start researching investments is which model best suits your needs. Here's a rundown of the pros and cons of each:

Facility-based businesses are brick-and-mortar ones; the customer usually goes to the business to buy a product or service. Examples would be a massage spa, retail store, tutoring center, gym, or a restaurant. Restaurant franchises might be large scale, with a full bar and extensive seating; fast food; or in a specialty category, such as frozen yogurt.

Within this category, *large retail* concepts are mainly found in large strip mall spaces or standalone buildings. They require substantial space, customized build-outs, and consequently, large investments. These companies carry recognized brand names and an established customer base.

Some facility-based businesses are considered *light retail*. These businesses fit well in strip mall locations, because they require a small footprint and less build-out. They also require a smaller investment than large retail franchises, since building costs and lease agreements tend to be lower.

Facility-Based Pros:

- There's plenty of opportunity for customer interaction.

- Advertising, signage, and business location combine to help bring customers to you.

- It's possible to operate many facility-based businesses as a semi-absentee owner by hiring a manager to run daily operations.

- This model can come with "franchise in a box" ease if the concept allows for quick build out and fast startup. For example, a martial arts franchise might be installed in a matter of weeks, because it doesn't take much time to put up mirrors, lay down mats, and install a counter.

Facility-Based Cons:

- The site selection process often involves a long lead time. After making a sizeable investment, a lengthy search process can significantly delay return on investment.

- Facility-based concepts can require a large amount of capital to get started and to run. You will need to build out the facility and, going forward, you will encounter fixed overhead costs such as rent, utilities, and long-term lease commitments.

- Once you commit to a site, your business becomes tethered there. Retail businesses tend to be about location, location, location, and getting just the right spot can make or break a startup. The success or failure of other businesses in your area has an impact on yours, good or bad. If you are in the right location, you might enjoy great success, but a poor choice could break your business.

- Your business may be open during weekends and holidays, and you will either have to be there or pay someone to be there for you.

Service-based businesses generally involve the service provider going to the customer's home. Examples include painting, cleaning services, home health aide providers, window covering companies, and even floor sales. Some of these are businesses can operate with low overhead. For example, painting and home inspection services are businesses in which the franchisee doesn't need a facility. Many of these opportunities can be run by the franchisee from anywhere, including from home.

Service-Based Pros:

- A service-based concept is almost always cheaper and faster to get off the ground than a facility-based concept. There are much lower financial barriers to entry.

- It's easy to scale a service-based business, so you can build it over time, adding staff as needed. This is sometimes as easy as adding crews or trucks.

- Your schedule may be more flexible because you are not necessarily bound to the operating hours of a store.

Service-Based Cons:

- It will take more work for customers to find you in your service-based business. The reality is that you will need to find them, utilizing community connections, advertising, word of mouth, and any other publicity or marketing tools available to you.

- In some cases, such as a home restoration business, you *are* the business, which does not allow for an absentee model. In this scenario, you are the artisan or the service provider, and your hands-on presence will be a key factor in your success.

SERVICE MODEL:
WHO IS YOUR CUSTOMER?

Up to this point, we have primarily been discussing *business-to-customer* franchise models (sometimes referred to as B2C in the industry). However, there is another category of concepts that are built around *business-to-business* (B2B) concepts. B2Bs are businesses that provide a product or service to other businesses. For example, restaurant owners must have their stove hoods cleaned on a quarterly basis to reduce the risk of fires—one B2B model might specialize in cleaning those hoods by setting up a rotating quarterly schedule for a whole territory of restaurants. Another business might produce high-quality graphics, wrapping logos around delivery vehicles or installing large-format graphic images on the sides of buildings. Just like a business-to-customer model, a business-to-business franchise can be facility-based, service-based, or a combination of both. Many combinations of those business models are possible.

LEVELS OF ENGAGEMENT:
HOW HANDS-ON DO YOU WANT TO BE?

The way a franchise business is built depends on the franchisee's level of engagement. The right model for you depends on your ambitions, your abilities, and your available capital. There are multiple levels of engagement to consider as you plan your path. One thing to keep in mind about all options, though, is that it's often possible to start the franchise process as a semi-absentee owner. If you are especially risk averse, unable to leave the shelter of a traditional job, or looking to choose a more hands-off opportunity, you can opt to make your entry point into franchising one that allows you to hold on to your "day job" as long as you choose. Last year, I worked with a candidate who already owns a business in one industry. He wanted to diversify his investments, and told me he could set aside ten to fifteen hours a week to give to a second business. We were able to find a perfect opportunity for him in a fitness franchise—one that allowed him to add his new business to his existing schedule, rather than trade one for the other.

Owner-Operator/Artisan Model

The most basic franchise format is an owner-operator model. With owner-operator businesses, the franchisee may be the artisan, the person behind the counter, or the one in the truck providing the service. In this case, the owner has one business, and probably one location. It is a great starting point for someone who has always dreamed of owning a business, and who wants to work for himself. Buying a franchise helps you get off the ground quickly with a new business. An owner-operator may be interested in building a good business, but is not necessarily interested in substantial growth or multiple locations. As an owner-operator, you will spend your time working *in* the business, not *on* the business. You will be tied to the facility or the truck, taking care of the daily needs of the business.

It can be challenging to accomplish the sales and marketing that drive growth if you are a full-time artisan. Some people find balance and happiness in this model, and some gradually cut down their hands-on time in favor of paid labor as they grow the business.

The Executive Model

The business owner who wants to leverage his or her capital to deliver the highest possible return on investment might consider the executive model. This person has the capital and business acumen to build a large operation. Over the long term, people choosing to leverage the executive model want to work *on* the business, not *in* the business. They will always be engaged, but not necessarily as the artisan or day-to-day operator. The franchise owner may spend ten, fifteen, twenty, or forty hours a week minding the business, focusing on the higher-level decisions. He or she might be considering the advertising plan for the coming months or focusing on putting the right managers in place to run various locations.

The executive model can be lucrative. At this level, you can take advantage of some economies of scale. As your business grows, you can focus on leading the managers of your locations, or setting up accounts to grow your service businesses. You still need to learn the business, of course, and you'll keep mindful eye on marketing and cash flow, but you will have managers to be in the store or drive the truck every day. For some investors, the ideal way to build a franchise business is to start out as an artisan, learning the work and bringing the business to profitability, and to eventually move to a more executive role.

STRATEGIC FRANCHISE OWNERSHIP:
BENEFITS OF GOING BIG

Beyond the basic franchise business models, we find strategic ownership—larger-scale franchise investments. If you want to build something bigger than a single unit, there are ways to strategically develop a significant business through franchise ownership. The idea is to build a sizeable business that, over time, can provide enough income to replace or exceed a corporate level income and provide a significant return on investment. The two major models for approaching this kind of plan are the *multi-unit model* and the *area development model*.

Multi-Unit Model

You know it's possible to invest in franchises one at a time. In this approach, you invest in a single XYZ franchise, and pay a single franchise fee—we'll work with $50,000 as an example. In this model, you open your XYZ franchise location eight months after signing the franchise agreement. When the business is stable twelve months later, you might go back to the franchisor and request a second XYZ franchise.

There are two potential disadvantages to investing one-at-a-time if your long-term goal in owning multiples. First, in most cases, you will have to pay another full franchise fee for a second location. In this example, you would pay another $50,000 fee. Second, assuming you invested in a growing franchise concept, the best locations in your area may have already been sold by the time you're ready to double down. If so, you'll be shut out from expanding your market.

In the multi-unit investment model, you invest up front for the rights to open multiple locations in strategic territories within a defined time period—but not necessarily right away. This is also known as a franchise development schedule.

The strategic investment strategy can be applied to service-based franchise concepts as well as facility-based models. Instead of investing in a small territory and hoping you can secure additional territory in the future, you invest in a large territory upfront, gaining the ability to scale the business to your desired level down the line—and protecting desirable locations.

There are three main benefits to signing a multi-unit franchise agreement. First, if you are investing in multiple franchise units up front, the franchisor will likely give you a discount on franchise fees for the additional units. For example, if the XYZ franchise fee for the first unit was $50,000, the second unit franchise fee may be $30,000, and the third unit fee may be $20,000. So instead of paying $100,000 in franchise fees for two franchise units purchased individually, with the multi-unit investment strategy you would acquire three for the same investment. Second, the strategy allows you to lock-up or protect territories for planned expansion. You'll be set up to expand when you are ready. Third, in the long run, with a multi-unit approach, you leverage your advertising and back-office support across multiple locations, making your marketing and administrative dollars go farther.

Area Development/Master Franchise Model

The second major strategic ownership approach is area development. In this model—sometimes called the master franchise—the franchisee buys the rights to a large geographic area. For example, you may buy the rights to develop a franchise concept for the state of Illinois or the city of Chicago. When I invested in a master franchise, I bought the rights to three states for a specific concept. An area developer or master franchisee works with the franchisor to find franchisees and help them set up their new businesses. As an area developer, your job is to work with the franchisor to identify franchisees for locations within a specific geographic area. When I bought the rights to multiple states, I helped the franchisor grow in those states, and I helped franchisees go into business and build their own operations.

As an area developer, you are essentially working as an independent agent of the franchisor, helping that company expand while building your own business. You also take some of the responsibility for training and developing the new franchisees within your territory.

Unlike most single-franchise outlet investors, area development franchisees generate revenue in multiple ways. First, when they help place franchisees, they receive a portion of the upfront franchise fee. For example, if the franchise fee is $30,000, the area developer payout share might be $15,000. Second, when the new franchisee is launched and supported, the area developer gets a portion of the franchisee's monthly royalty payment to the franchisor. For example, if the franchisee is required to pay a percentage of monthly gross revenues as royalty payment, the area developer's share of the royalty may be half of that, or 2.5 percent. Third, many area developers have the right to open their own operating franchise units within their master territories to generate additional revenues and cash flow.

Area development is not for the faint of heart; this approach tends to require large capital investments, and the strategy may take a long while to grow to a significantly sized business. Good area development franchise opportunities are also hard to find. The advantage of building your business this way, though, is that in the long run, you will be paid for other people's work. You can create a steady revenue stream without direct responsibility for day-to-day operations. The initial investment may be large, but the end result is a wealth-building opportunity that works without your constant supervision.

DON'T MAKE THIS MISTAKE:
UNDERESTIMATING THE POWER OF THE BUSINESS MODEL

The strengths of the business model you invest in, and how well the model matches your abilities, are even more important than the product or service. You might love photography, but opening a photography studio under a faulty business model could be a recipe for disaster. As you navigate your investment options, keep sight of the structure and level of engagement you've chosen, the future goals you've set for yourself, and the professional strengths you bring to the table. If an option jibes with all of those, then ask yourself, "Does this model make sense to me? Can I see a way for both proprietor and customer to be satisfied at the end of any given transaction?" Steer clear of any model that doesn't quite click when you think it through—if you can't appreciate it as a win/win concept for everyone involved, then you probably aren't looking at a winning investment.

HOW FRANCHISING PAYS YOU

As the owner of a startup business, you're going to start out spending working capital—money you've set aside to live on and run your business with until it becomes profitable. In time, you can expect to reach a point where your business breaks even, when you'll have more cash coming in than going out. When that happens, the business becomes self-sustaining.

As the owner of that self-sustaining enterprise, you will have the freedom to decide how to spend the cash flow from your business. You may use profits to pay down debt or reinvest in the business for expansion or improvement. You may put away money for your retirement. You may pay yourself a salary. You may take a draw on your profits as a reward for your hard work.

Typically, a franchisee starts out paying his or herself a small salary, but as the business takes off, that salary can grow to replace corporate income. But there's another factor at work here that sets the business owner apart. As the business becomes profitable and pays the owner, it becomes not just a source of income, but a valuable asset in its own right.

Consider this chart that demonstrates one possible hypothetical combination of parallel paths for the investor who stays in a corporate job vs. one who invests in his or her own business:

FACTORING IN THE VALUE OF YOUR BUSINESS		
	Corporate Executive	vs. Franchise Owner
Year 1	$100,000 Salary	$0 Salary
Year 2	$103,000 Salary	$50,000 Salary
Year 3	$106,000 Salary	$100,000 Salary
Year 4	$109,000 Salary	$125,000 Salary
Year 5	$112,000 Salary	$150,000 Salary
5-Year Salary Total:	$530,000	$425,000
5-Year Asset Check:	$0 asset value of job	$450,000 asset value of franchise
Total Value	$530,000	$875,000

After five years of hard work in the corporate world, our executive has made a steady salary with regular raises. The franchise owner, on the other hand, sacrificed salary early on to build his business. But as the years pass, the balance sheets for these two individuals move in very different directions, with the biggest difference visible in that bottom line. The business has become much more than a job—it's become a source not just of income, but also of income security. And if you are the owner of that business, no one can come in to your office one day and say, "I'm sorry. You're not the guy anymore."

SUCCESS STORY:
ONE CORPORATE LETDOWN TOO MANY

Background: Harold's father worked for a Texas bakery for forty years, and Harold followed his dad into the business when he was just sixteen, loading trucks as a student and later, after earning his degree, working his way up through the sales department. When he was passed over for an upper-management promotion for a member of the owner's family, Harold moved on to another food company. After several years of exemplary work, he was let go and forced to reconsider his career path yet again.

Search Process: Harold didn't want to move on to another company that would undervalue his contributions, and so he decided to invest in a business that would utilize his ability to build new businesses, assess troubled programs, and assemble and lead strong, solutions-oriented teams. He considered consulting, but after several months of fruitlessly searching for the right opportunity, Harold began working with a franchise consultant.

Decision: Harold invested in a turn-key franchise that installs individual salon suites in shopping center spaces.

Result: "You could work for a company for twelve or thirteen years, build hundreds of millions of dollars in business, only to be shown the door," Harold says. "I'd rather be in control of my own destiny. I was not as concerned about the overall risk, because I felt like if I did the appropriate due diligence, I wanted my success to be dependent on me."

Best Advice: You can do as a great job as anybody can do, but when a company has taken all they need from you, they can still show you the door. How many times do you want to do that? Sometimes it's just better to take a risk on yourself.

CHAPTER SUMMARY

- Franchising touches nearly every industry, and there are thousands of business models available for an investor to consider. New concepts are being created all the time.

- Franchises generally fall into two categories, *facility-based* businesses where customers come to you, and *service-based* businesses, where you go to the customer.

- You'll need to decide if you want to be an owner/operator of your franchise business, or if you want to be an executive owner, hiring others to do the day-to-day work.

- For some investors, owning and operating one store or business is exactly right for their personal goals and lifestyles. For entrepreneurs and experienced executives who want to build a larger business, there are significant advantages to the multi-unit ownership franchise model.

THE NEXT STEP:

Go to the **HIRE YOURSELF** *resource page to learn more and take action*

QUIZ:
Choosing the Best Franchise Structure for You

WORKSHEET:
How Franchising Pays You: Job Value vs. Franchise Ownership Value

Go To:
HIREYOURSELFBOOK.COM/Resources

PART II

FINDING YOUR IDEAL FRANCHISE INVESTMENT

CHAPTER 4

KNOW WHAT YOU WANT: GOALS AND STRENGTHS

"If passion drives you, let reason hold the reins."

—BENJAMIN FRANKLIN

I f you'd asked me fifteen, twenty, or even twenty-five years ago what kind of business I'd like to run one day, I wouldn't have hesitated with my answer: A car dealership! It would have been an easy response, because both my father and my grandfather were Ford dealers. I practically grew up on a car lot, doing every job a kid can be given to help out behind the scenes. Because of that childhood, and because I've always been a little bit spellbound by the beauty and potential of a new car, I love the industry.

But I'm not a car dealer—as much as I love the idea of it, an automobile franchise was not the right business concept for me, and I'm glad I was level-headed enough to recognize that fact. There are a million reasons why a franchise concept that sounds like it's just your cup of tea can still be the wrong option. Making an informed choice about the industry and business model you want to pursue—and how you can succeed at it—is the cornerstone of solid franchise investment.

So often, I meet with a new candidate who tells me in our first conversation that he or she is planning to invest in a specific franchise concept, like XYZ Sub Shop. The candidate's reasoning seems sensible, something along the lines of, "People have to eat," or, "The ABC by my house is always busy." It's certainly true that choosing a franchise that meets a need and experiences a high level of demand makes good business sense. But what else matters? How about the business model? Or how the franchisee spends his or her days? Or how long it will take to break even, and what kind of profits a franchisee can expect to earn?

It's important to remember that just because a particular franchise is a *good* investment, doesn't mean it's necessarily the *right* investment for you.

Over the next three chapters, I'll walk you through steps you can follow to sift through your own priorities and then through the thousands of franchise choices available. My best advice as you set out to investigate the possibilities, and perhaps work with a consultant to narrow the field, is simply this: Keep an open mind. Look at each prospect with fresh eyes. In all likelihood, there's an investment out there that's perfect for you. The challenge is finding that gem in a mountain of other options—and recognizing it when you see it.

Your first step in finding your perfect franchise is identifying your own goals, needs, and strengths:

KNOW WHAT YOU WANT

Every candidate wants a business that offers a good return on investment. That's the shared bottom line for all of us. Beyond that, though, our goals are widely varied. Some investors are all about mining for higher margins. Some focus on the most efficient use of their capital. Some want a business that will be simple to operate. Some require great long-term growth potential. Some may be willing to give fifty or sixty hours a week to make a new business hum and succeed—but others are investing in a semi-absentee business primarily as a means to build a bridge *out* of their sixty-hour work weeks. The most important thing to do at the outset of your franchise search is figure out *why* you want to invest in your own business—and *what* you want to accomplish by doing so.

Think about your personal and professional goals, for the short term and the long, and how you see franchise investment as a means to accomplish them. I recommend writing out a short list of your priorities, based on your answers for each of the topics below. Once you've worked through what's important to you, use compatibility with your list as the first litmus test for any franchise of interest:

- *Engagement:* How engaged in your business do you want to be, up front and long term? Full time? Semi-absentee? Do you want to learn your business hands-on? If so, do you expect to transition those responsibilities to employees in the long term? Or do you want to remain the artisan, providing service yourself?

Some candidates may be willing to give fifty or sixty hours a week to make a new business hum and succeed—but others are investing in a semi-absentee business primarily as a means to build a bridge out of their sixty-hour work weeks.

- *Progression:* Are you building a bridge out of the corporate world or into retirement? And if so, how long do you want to keep your "day job" before transitioning to spending more time on your franchise and less (or none) on someone else's corporate achievements?

- *Growth:* Do you want to scale the business over time, adding more crews or trucks or opening multiple locations? Do you see your initial investment as the first of many?

- *Income:* How much income do you need to create with your franchise investment? Will a single unit be enough to meet your financial requirements? In addition to the salary you pay yourself, do you expect your investment to become a valuable asset that you can someday sell or transition to family members?

- *Location:* Where do you want to be—now and in the long term? Does this information impact where you open your business? Geographically, where's the sweet spot for you? Sometimes the perfect franchise business isn't available where you want to be.

- *Status:* How important is the status of the business to you? Would you be embarrassed, for example, to own a port-a-potty franchise? How closely do you want to associate yourself with the business you buy? Is there a role you hope your business will play in the community?

- *Family:* How do the needs and wants of the people you love fit into your vision of franchise ownership? Do you want your family to have a direct role in your business?

- *Schedule:* Do you hope to choose an investment that allows you to spend more time at home? How do you feel about working weekends? Or nights? Or holidays? Does your ideal business require hands-on management on-demand, during bankers' hours, or even 24/7?

- *Purpose:* Do you want to make a difference in others' lives, develop and grow employees, and/or provide a beneficial product or service to customers? How important is it to you to feel like you're making a worthwhile contribution with your choice of business?

> *Filtering franchise choices through your goals list will help keep you focused on what you want to accomplish and how you want to get there.*

- *Risk Tolerance:* How do you plan to capitalize the business? Are you willing to leverage your retirement savings or equity in your home? Are you open to personally guaranteeing a business loan or a five-year property lease? What is your tolerance to risk and how will that define your investment threshold?

- *Duration:* How long do you want to own the business? Do you have an exit plan?

Now let's go back to the XYZ Sub Shop and the investor who's willing to put his or her life savings into it on the basis that people always have to eat. That reasoning, or the reasoning that XYZ is often busy, isn't enough to go on—not even close. An investor needs to know how XYZ fits with the answers to *each* of these goal questions. Use them to screen your first impulses, and also the investments friends and colleagues tell you about. Filtering franchise choices through your goals list will help keep you focused on what you want to accomplish and how you want to get there.

KNOW YOUR SKILLS AND STRENGTHS

Think for a minute about your personnel file with your current or most recent employer, about your greatest professional successes, about the work you've done that's made a difference for your department or your company or your own business. We all have talents and abilities that stand out—having a firm handle on yours will help you make smart choices as you look at investments. This is not the time to make emotional decisions—it's a time to match needs and strengths for the best possible outcome.

Whatever your personal and professional defining characteristics, the right business model with a successful franchisor may be able to help leverage your skills *and* compensate for your weaknesses. Franchise systems are designed to help each investor succeed. The key, as you ask yourself the questions below, is to clearly identify the areas where you're likely to shine, and to flag those where you know you're going to need extra support. Consider each business model against those criteria—your conclusions may surprise you.

- What is your level of success in sales? Are you good at it? Do you enjoy it? Would doing business development sales ten hours a day be torture for you, or would you enjoy being out in the community telling customers about the great value of the product or service your company offers?

- How are your people-management skills? How do you feel about managing employees? Do you want any at all? Could you comfortably manage a small staff—or a large one? Do you want to be able to hire a manager to do that for you? Are you a strong communicator and a capable motivator? Is important to you to make a difference in your employees' personal and professional grow while being part of your business?

- What kind of business acumen do you bring to the table at the outset of your business? Do you have experience with and a knack for running multi-faceted business units? Are you a marketing whiz looking for a new challenge? Are you able to read a financial statement and understand it? Numbers are the language of business, and you'll have an important skill going in if you're already good at interpreting them.

- What's your comfort level with changing technology? Some terrific franchise opportunities come bundled with state of the art tech systems (and excellent training in how to use them). If you don't have a natural aptitude for that kind of thing, are you trainable and willing to learn?

- What kinds of personal and professional contacts and connections can you leverage to help build your business? Are you well connected in your community and/or in the industry you are considering?

- Do you have a particular skill that might lend itself to a franchise of interest? For example, are you a certified teacher looking to open a tutoring center? If so, that's wonderful—but do you also have experience and skills compatible with running the business end of the franchise? Are you willing to leverage all the skills you developed working for someone else to run your own business?

It's important to remember that just because a particular franchise is a good investment doesn't mean it's necessarily the right investment for you.

KEEP PERSONAL INTERESTS IN THEIR PLACE

You don't necessarily need to know the industry you invest in on a professional level, but it helps if it's something of interest to you. On the other hand, just because you like to craft, that pottery painting franchise could be wrong for you if the business model doesn't set you up for success. I always ask my candidates about their personal interests and hobbies—Do they work out? Do they like working with their hands? Do they travel?—but these questions are more to get a sense of the person than they are to inform an investment choice. The fact is that what you're interested in during your leisure time has very little bearing on what business might best suit your talents. Think of it as the difference between what you like and what you're good at—I may love a good glass of wine, but that doesn't mean I'd be a good vintner, or even a good wine steward. I may like baseball, but you'll never see me running a memorabilia shop at Wrigley Field.

Even though you need to keep some clarity between what you enjoy and what you're good at, there are some general areas of interest that can help inform franchise selection. For example:

- Are you outgoing? Do you feel comfortable or even energized when you interact with strangers for the first time? Or are you more of an introvert?

- Do you like a challenge? Do you rise to the occasion when you take on something new and unfamiliar?

- Are you good at mental math? No—I'm not talking about calculus or trigonometry here—but about the knack for business numbers I often find strong candidates share.

- Is it important to you to make a difference in other people's lives? Some candidates do particularly well when they find a franchise that lines up nicely with their desire to make a difference in others' lives.

When you sit down with a franchise consultant or your list of franchise concepts of interest, be self-aware. Don't be the investor who comes to me and says, "I like animals [or tea, or computers, or massage] . . . What do you have in that?" Instead, try leading with your abilities, perhaps something like this:

- "I'm a great team leader with a gift for motivating people."

- "I've won two major marketing awards in the last decade."

- "I've had my best professional successes when I've had the freedom to set my own schedule."

- "I do my best work when I feel like the end result matters, like I'm providing a service that is really helping the customer."

Any of those openers would give you a great place to start.

DON'T MAKE THIS MISTAKE:
INVESTING IN YOUR HOBBY

In my experience, business and hobbies make a poor mix. All too often, when a candidate turns a hobby into a business, it becomes work, plain and simple—and the joy goes right out of it.

I often think of a story in the book *The E-Myth Revisited* by Michael Gerber, about a woman with a passion for baking and a sheaf of wonderful family recipes. Her impulse was to take this passion and turn it into a business, so she opened a bakery. Unfortunately, the reality of running the business overwhelmed her passion, and she found she no longer cared much for either.

Hobbies, by definition, are not work—they're the pursuit of interests you find inspiring, or invigorating, or relaxing. We all need these escapes from the stresses of daily life, so try to keep them separate from investment decisions. With a little luck and a lot of hard work, a wisely chosen franchise may soon free you up to spend more time pursuing your hobbies—and you want to still find joy in them when that day comes.

EXPLORING YOUR OPTIONS

Now that you have assessed your goals, skills, and interests, the next step is to start researching unique franchise concepts. There are thousands of franchise businesses available, but, of course, they're not all good ones. How do you sort through and separate the gems from the coal?

Most people start with the Internet. Often, when I complete my research and present the franchise concepts to a candidate, I can hear them typing into a search engine even while we're still on the phone. If you're working on your own and search, for instance, for a home-cleaning franchise, hundreds of results will pop up. You need a system to weed the proven concepts from the riskier ones. The way I look at it, there are three primary ways to go through this process. For our purposes, we can call them Good, Better, and Best.

Good: Fishing for Information.

You can go to a website that advertises franchising concepts and provide your personal information there. Franchise companies may pay to advertise on this site, and third-party salespeople will likely purchase your contact information from the site and reach out to you to offer you more details. This can quickly become intrusive and overwhelming, so proceed with caution when deciding where you want to provide your personal information. Using this kind of franchise portal can be a regrettable experience that leaves you inundated with phone calls and emails from now until eternity—not just from the people you gave your name to, but also from everyone they'll sell your information to, as well.

Better: Straight to the Sales Department.

To find out more about a particular company, you can also go straight to the source, to the franchise company. You may have an interest in a particular brand, or you may have read about a prospect you want to explore in a business magazine like *SUCCESS, Entrepreneur,* or *Forbes.* When you approach the franchisor directly, you come to them as an "organic lead." If you visit a franchise's home page, you will find an information tab. You can click on that tab and provide your contact information and request to learn more about franchise opportunities. By doing so, you enter the company's sales pipeline, and someone in their franchise development group will certainly respond. However, there's no financial benefit to you to going directly through a franchisor's website to request information. The franchise fee described does not depend upon how you were registered or introduced to the company. The drawback to this approach is that it tends to be narrow. It is challenging to compare concepts when each is being "sold" to you directly from the franchise company.

Best: Enlisting a Neutral Third Party.

The third alternative is to engage a neutral third party to compile information and help you evaluate the different concepts. That neutral party is—you guessed it!—the franchise consultant. A good consultant has broad experience and expertise in the franchise world and can walk you through a self-evaluation and investment search. A good franchise consultant will research concepts for you, and introduce you to the options that best match your goals and strengths. A consultant can take some of the emotion out of the decision and help you recognize when a concept is made more of whiz-bang marketing than proven success in practice.

When you do choose a concept to learn more about, a franchise consultant brings you to the franchisor not as an unknown entity with an interest in investment, but as a vetted candidate. As I noted in Chapter 1, most good franchise consultants offer their services at "no charge" to their candidates. Many people ask me how franchise consultants are compensated for their services, and the answer is that they are paid a referral fee by the franchisor when a candidate invests. This is very similar to the way a realtor is paid. Why do franchisors pay for this service? Because they, too, are trying to find not just any partner, but the right partner. They build trusting relationships with consultants who bring solid, solvent, vetted candidates to the table.

SUCCESS STORY:
AN EXIT FROM THE SPEEDWAY LIFESTYLE

Background: Dave came to franchise investment not from the world of corporate suits, but from a career in NASCAR racing. He'd driven, owned race teams, consulted, and built his own business building car chassis. After years of following the circuit from city to city, though, Dave and his wife were getting tired of the constant travel his job required. They wanted to find a business that could replace some racing industry income—without requiring them to be on the spot all the time.

Search Process: "When we first started to research," Dave says, "it was kind of mind-boggling to be able to figure out who is making money, who's not, and where a business's profitability is." He met with me and after our interview I helped him find four prospective companies to look at: an auto repair company, a locksmith company, a frozen yogurt franchise, and a window-cleaning company.

Decision: Dave bought the window-cleaning franchise. Even though it was the last of the prospects he considered, it turned out to be the best fit with its relatively low entry level and low risk. It's not a big operation, so it wasn't a huge time commitment.

Result: Dave and his wife are really just getting started and building a customer base. They're nearly at a break-even point, and hope to be bringing in a regular income from the business in a year.

They have one full-time manager/salesman and two part-time employees.

Best Advice: "With a franchise," Dave says, "the thing that makes sense to me is you're buying a system. You're buying somebody's success. We did extensive research talking with other franchisees. Some of them are successful now, but struggled in the beginning. Just about everyone that struggled didn't follow the system. The franchisor knows how to make money, and how to control costs. I say just follow their system—and the process has been very seamless for us."

_____

CHAPTER SUMMARY

- The most important thing to do at the outset of your franchise search is understand your own motivations and goals. Assess every franchise concept through the filter of those things that matter most to you.

- When it comes to choosing a business concept, maintain the perspective of an investor and a savvy executive—not that of a once or future consumer.

- Look for a concept that will utilize the business experience and strengths you already have.

- With thousands of franchise options to sort through, you might find it helpful to speak with a franchise consultant who can help you separate legitimate prospects from those that are either ill-suited to your needs, goals, and talents—or not worthy of your investment.

THE NEXT STEP:

Go to the **HIRE YOURSELF** *resource page to learn more and take action*

QUIZ:
What Matters Most to You? Creating a Filter for Franchise Concepts

WORKSHEET:
Identify your Strengths and Weaknesses

Go To:
HIREYOURSELFBOOK.COM/Resources

CHAPTER 5

MEETING YOUR MATCH: THE RIGHT CONCEPT AND BUSINESS SYSTEMS

"I feel that luck is preparation meeting opportunity."

—OPRAH WINFREY

From corporate culture and management style to sheer scope and strength, franchises come in all different shapes and sizes. Some franchise groups feel almost like a family—the original founders may still be involved, and the company may be tightly knit with a high level of engagement. Others can feel more regimented, living and breathing by precision measurements of pretty much everything. Many leave nothing to chance; a few are more open to variation, to letting franchisees have more choice in what they stock or the variety of services they provide.

I sometimes tell my candidates that sifting through all the myriad tangible and intangible aspects of each franchisor can feel a lot like choosing a college for a son or daughter. You want to know if it's too big or too small; if it's overly highbrow or too casual to take seriously; if it's safe; if you'll be making a good investment in your family's future. There are countless factors that weigh into the decision about which place is just right for your child, and so it is with finding a reputable, profitable, compatible franchise.

How do you know when you've found "the one"? When you find a great concept tied to an outstanding business model, you'll know you're on the right track. In this chapter, we'll explore how to narrow a field of thousands of franchise possibilities down to the chosen few you'll deem deserving of detailed investigation.

THE CONCEPT

At every successive stage of choosing a franchise, you'll get a closer look at how each operates. In the early stages, when you're reading up, Googling like mad, and/or working with a franchise consultant to narrow a field of thousands of possibilities down to a few to investigate in depth, you're looking for two main components: a solid concept and proven business systems.

Concept often colors your very first test of a franchisor. You ask the question, "What do they do?" and the answer to that question is the concept. This can be anything from *bakery* to *business coach* to *painting franchise* to *gym*. The possibilities are endless. Once you know what the company does, the next question is about who it serves—so your answers above might become *gourmet bakery* and *executive business coach, commercial painting franchise,* and *women's-only gym.* Beyond the market designation, a franchise might have a unique hook or angle that sets it apart—for example, the bakery might specialize in cupcakes or offer delivery; the business coach might specialize in a unique hiring process for finding "A players"; the painting franchise might leverage patented technology in its process; and the gym might build its schedule with super-efficient thirty-minute classes. In each case, there's some defining characteristic that helps set the business apart.

As consumers, we're aware of concept already; but as a potential investor, you're looking closer, at what makes a concept unique, how it's implemented, and how it provides a satisfying experience to the customer. What makes our bakery better than XYZ Bakery that's been in business half a mile away for decades? And what does that gym offer its clientele to maintain their loyalty when there are so many other fitness businesses around? As an investor, you want to know what makes the franchise tick.

As you search franchise opportunities, you may choose to eliminate whole sectors of candidates based on industry and concept. For example, some people have no interest in working in the food industry—thus taking several hundred franchise possibilities out of the running. Some don't want to be responsible for a retail outlet and the investment that entails—and there goes another huge sector. It's fine to set clear parameters regarding what kind of businesses you *don't* want to consider, but be careful about dismissing too many possibilities out of hand. In my experience with investment candidates, after they've gotten up close and personal with a few well-chosen franchise concepts, many choose the option that was their last choice before digging in and learning more.

The key at this early stage is being able to identify a concept that benefits everyone involved: the franchisor has a winning idea that grows and makes money; the franchisee finds a way to leverage his or her business acumen to help further build the business and earn profits; and the customer receives a beneficial service or product.

If a franchise's concept exhibits this win/win/win design and seems solid and logical to you, then it's time to move on to the next measure of assessment: the business system.

THE BUSINESS SYSTEM

The second main question you should ask when looking at franchise investments is, "How does the franchisor provide its product in a way that it can replicate success in each new unit?"

When we talk about these systems, we're talking about how the franchising company accomplishes everything that happens in the business. How do they do hiring, training, purchasing, marketing, product delivery, billing? What technology is implemented in these processes? As you gain more knowledge of individual companies, you can—and should—be impressed by the efficiency and comprehensiveness of their systems. Great franchises leave little to chance—they have all the steps to success broken down into simple, meaningful, and clear processes. And those steps mean that you should be able to see the uniformity from one unit to the next, or experience it in terms of marketing, responsiveness, product offerings, and professionalism, if the company provides a service.

You won't be privy to the inner workings of a franchisor's systems at first glance, but you should be able to get a sense of efficiency and capability in any interaction with the company. Can you appreciate how the franchisor, franchisee, and customer are in a win/win/win triangle? Do you feel like you could count on this company if you were a customer or client? What about as a franchisee? If so, think about where your confidence comes from: I'd be willing to bet it's rooted in the systems the franchisor has in place to ensure quality and consistency from each franchisee.

> *Great franchises leave little to chance—they have all the steps to success broken down into simple, meaningful, and clear processes.*

MORE TO CONSIDER

When you find a number of franchise opportunities that are appealing in terms of both concept and business systems, then you can turn your attention to other factors that add to or take away from their appeal. Ideally, after you've worked through each of these characteristics, you'll narrow your way to just three or four companies to fully investigate using the steps outlined in Chapter 6. How does each of your companies of interest measure up in these areas?

Training

Every franchisor has a unique approach to training, and, in some cases, the more you invest the more help you're likely to receive. Many businesses have stellar plans in place for getting you up to speed—and up and running. Consider 5 Guys Burgers and Fries, which has seen all its U.S. franchise licenses snapped up over the past several years. One of the things that helped create its success was its model of sending an all-pro support team out for onsite training and the launch of each individual unit.

In this business, I've had the opportunity to see companies that offer bare-bones training for their franchisees and those that deliver five-star classroom and onsite instruction. Is there a correlation between training and success? Often there is, though certainly not always. No amount of training can compensate for an inferior product, a flawed business system, or a terrible location. But when things are equal, great training is a huge plus.

No franchisor is going to spell out every detail of its training program to an investor who's still in the window-shopping stage, but with a little research, you can often get a good sense of whether a company considers training to be a key piece of its franchisees' paths to success.

> *Is there a correlation between training and success? Often, but no amount of training can compensate for an inferior product, a flawed business system, or a terrible location.*

Image

One of the great advantages of buying into an established franchise is brand recognition. As a franchisee, you don't have to start at square one to prove that Brand A sells good stuff or great service at a fair price—the franchisor has already done that for you. The value in being able to put on the mantle of trust, reliability, excellence, friendly service—whatever Brand A is associated with—is a big part of what you're paying for.

If you become a franchisee, you'll be entrusted with upholding the good reputation of the brand and keeping its image polished to a shine. Be sure you believe you'd be up to that task.

Some companies' images stick with a generic and positive professionalism. Others are more complex. They may cater to a certain demographic; and they may present themselves as hip, smart, ethical, posh, practical, fanciful, or parental—you name it. At this stage, all you need to consider is whether you feel comfortable with the image a targeted company presents. You don't need to be a cookie-cutter copy of the CEO or another franchisee, but you need to feel that you, too, could represent Brand A.

Know that down the line, if you take things a step further with these companies, folks on the other side of the table will also be wondering how you might represent the image—their image—to the world.

In addition to the positive, and sometimes quirky, aspects of image, some companies have underlying issues or problems. No company is perfect, and I doubt many exist with no complaints. That said, as you research your companies, tune in to complaint trends that are especially aggressive or widespread. It's hard to underestimate the value of reputation. In this day and age, with new review sites popping up every day and social media playing an increasing role in consumer choice, it's easier than ever to spot a mark on a good name you're thinking of investing in.

Of course, you can't believe everything you read on the Internet. If you think you see a problem with a company's image or reputation, take the time to follow up and learn more. The point of this exercise isn't to scratch any company that's ever had a complaint from your list; it's becoming aware of any issues that might affect corporate image.

The Size of the System

When it comes to looking at the size of a franchisor, there's no right or wrong measure. Instead, you're looking for an organization that feels like a good fit for you. Lately, I've been talking about colleges with my son and am reminded again of the parallels to choosing a franchise investment. I asked him to think about whether he'd rather get the sense that he's a small fish in a big pond or a big fish in a small pond—there are good arguments for either position.

In general, franchisors are masters of right-sizing their businesses—it's one of the factors that distinguish the good companies from the great. You can find terrific companies with just a hundred franchisees and you can find great companies that have twenty-five hundred or more. At the end of the day, this is a personal decision, based on your comfort level.

Up and Coming, or Firmly Established?

Hand in hand with the question of what size business is comfortable for you is the question of whether you're interested in getting in on the ground floor of something that's just beginning to grow, or if you want a business that's paid its dues and earned widespread brand recognition. These questions are about much more than just what feels right to you—they're also directly tied to your level of investment and your tolerance for risk.

Do you want a concept that's been around for thirty years and is proven? You'll be making the safest possible bet if you do. And even if a concept has a thousand franchisees, it can still be growing and thriving. That said, there are potential drawbacks. First and foremost, you'll pay a premium for an established track record. Second, when a great concept gains a solid foothold, competitors sometimes spring up with a new spin on the same good idea, potentially changing the market. Third, the best territories may already be taken.

On the other hand, do you want to be an early adopter—one of the first to invest in a great concept? You'll be able to get a great deal and have your pick of territories—but you'll also have to live with the uncertainty of not knowing if the franchisor will grow gracefully or burn itself out by trying to fly too fast and too high.

This is one of the trickiest decisions a franchisee candidate has to consider. It's also an area where a good franchise consultant can offer some unique and valuable insight. A fairly new concept that's doing well and growing smart is likely to be a known quantity to a franchise investment insider long before it's making the business news or expanding across the country. In addition, consultant groups like FranChoice and some individual franchise consultants meet with the leadership teams of up-and-coming franchises, review their financials, and check their backgrounds to vet them before considering them for the candidates they work with. This vetting process can mercifully take some of the mystery out of your assessment of an unknown franchisor.

I advise my candidates to stick with vetted concepts that are well capitalized and responsibly run. Within those parameters, though, there's a vast range of risk between the up-and-coming concepts and the old guard, blue chip options. The bottom line is this: There's a lot of merit in going with a proven concept, but there's great potential in being an early adopter of an idea that's just starting to take off. Only you can decide where your risk tolerance lies.

Feel-Good Franchises

If you're looking to connect in your community, to give back to society, to share a special gift or talent, there may be a perfect franchise for you. Some companies emphasize ethics and altruism in many aspects of their operations by prioritizing their roles as good corporate citizens; choosing environmentally friendly operating procedures; and/or fostering personal development and growth in their employees. As you read about individual franchisors, this information sometimes bubbles to the top and makes one company stand out in an industry or region—especially if part of your motivation for going out on your own is to escape a corporation you've come to consider soulless.

In addition to corporate commitment to philanthropy or ethical operations, some businesses are, by design, built to help people. If this is important to you, there are countless options that you might find appealing. Among these are businesses that enlighten and educate children, businesses that help provide care for the elderly and the infirm, and businesses that help their clients improve their health and well-being.

If you want to make a difference—and a great many of my candidates do—there are some truly rewarding franchise concepts available for you.

Communication

When you're considering buying a franchise, you're weighing the risks and benefits of entering into a long-term relationship with the franchisor—most likely for ten years or more. That's a huge commitment. The relationship is one that some sometimes gets complicated—what senior partner/junior partner relationship isn't? It's important that you feel comfortable with the franchisor you choose—and that you feel communication between you is clear and effective.

In these early stages, when you're still exploring all your options, look for companies that clearly articulate their goals and plans; executives who are both knowledgeable and relatable—even if only in their press quotes; and—if you have access to them—franchisees who seem happy and confident.

As you move through later stages of investigation, keep communication in mind—make sure you're partnering with a company that seems responsive and positive.

Look and Feel

Not every franchise you have an interest in is going to be available for you to put to a real "sniff test," but there's no substitute for seeing a business in action. If an outpost of a franchise you've got your eye on is open to the public, stop by as a customer and soak it in. Get an idea how many people go in and out. See if the employees are cheerful, helpful, and knowledgeable.

If a company provides a service, consider trying it out. Maybe it's high time to re-grout your shower or take your kid to get yogurt or accept a free trial at a gym. When you can, use your five senses—and that elusive sixth sense—and listen to what they're telling you about the business.

> *If you want to make a difference—and a great many of my candidates do—there are some truly rewarding franchise concepts available for you.*

DON'T MAKE THIS MISTAKE:
INVESTING IN AN UNVETTED CONCEPT

Almost without exception, I advise my candidates to go with a thoroughly vetted franchise concept. That means looking for a franchise concept with a solid, established brand that's growing *or* choosing to be an early adopter of a concept that's been carefully vetted by a reputable and knowledgeable franchise consultant.

You may find yourself tempted by a low price, the "cool" factor of a novel concept, or the idea of getting in the ground floor, but be sure you've done your homework and made sure any franchisor you're considering entrusting your money to is well-run and well-capitalized. A rash investment could lead to a windfall success, but it could also lead to disaster. You're not playing the lottery here—you're making a much bigger commitment, and you owe it to yourself to rely on good research over any other factor.

SUCCESS STORY:
MARTIALING THE COURAGE TO MAKE A CHANGE

Background: Mike had always been in public relations and marketing—promoting people and companies and helping them grow. For twenty years, he toyed with the idea of working for himself, but never made a move. When he was downsized by his company, he took it as the shove he needed to start a new chapter in his life.

Search Process: Mike liked the idea of the support that comes with buying a franchise, and as he researched he paid close attention to which companies provided strong operations support and good brand recognition. He and his wife had a particular interest in choosing a franchise that would play a positive role in their community. He worked with me to find an opportunity that would fill that need.

Decision: Mike invested in a martial arts franchise that emphasizes character development and anti-bullying along with teaching basic skills. He was so committed to the concept and convinced of its success that he leveraged his 401(k) fund to buy the business.

Result: "For me," Mike says, "the ultimate upside to any business, beyond revenues you might make, is the impact you can have on your customers, your community, and your family. Here was an opportunity for us to not only go into business ourselves, but to do something positive for kids, too."

Best Advice: "If you would have told me a year ago that I'd be looking to open a series of martial arts schools, I'd have said you were crazy," Mike says. "The best piece of advice I could give a potential franchisee is to be open to unexpected opportunities. My business is going to be my retirement, my future, and I might have missed out on it if I hadn't kept an open mind."

CHAPTER SUMMARY

- When you find a great win/win/win concept tied to an outstanding business model, you'll know you're on the right track.

- Great franchises have success broken down into efficient, meaningful steps—and those steps allow them to replicate success from one unit to the next.

- A big part of choosing the right franchise for you is finding a company you can see yourself in a long-term relationship with. Look at characteristics like corporate culture, communications, and stage of development to help you assess the elusive factors that make a company a good potential partner.

THE NEXT STEP:

Go to the **HIRE YOURSELF** *resource page to learn more and take action*

QUIZ:

Identifying a Great Concept: What's the Win/Win/Win?

WORKSHEET:

Business Systems Assessment

WORKSHEET:

Training and Support Assessment

Go To:

HIREYOURSELFBOOK.COM/Resources

CHAPTER 6

FINDING "THE ONE": INVESTIGATING THE TOP FRANCHISE CONCEPTS FOR YOU

"Far and away the best prize that life offers is the chance to work hard at work worth doing."

—THEODORE ROOSEVELT

I n the previous chapters, you identified what you want and need in a franchise investment, and then used factors ranging from concept to corporate personality to narrow the field from thousands of options to hundreds, to, I hope at this point, just a few contenders. These are the companies that meet all of your minimum requirements, offer franchise ownerships that are in line with your goals, and pass a cursory assessment of concept, business systems, and compatibility. You may have whittled the list down on your own, or done so with the advice and guidance of a consultant, but now it's time to dig deeper and really get to know the companies on your short list.

I help my candidates focus down to three or four contenders, and I suggest you, too, weed out unsuitable options until you get to a very few. From this point on, your research will be more time intensive, and three or four companies are plenty to take through a deeper investigation.

There are four core franchise investigation steps laid out in some detail in this chapter. It's possible you'll eliminate a company at the first step, or the second, or the last. Even if you go all the way to Step Four with each short-list company, at the end of your investigation, you should have plenty of information to make an informed and confident choice.

The discovery process will put you in direct contact with the companies on your list. You can expect the whole investigation process to take four to six weeks.

INVESTIGATION STEP ONE:
INTRODUCTION CALL OR WEBINAR

The introduction call marks your first real conversation with the franchisor's representative. In some cases, this will be a person who specializes in franchise development, and in other cases it could be the company's CEO. If you've worked with a franchise consultant, that person will help arrange this call, and will have recommended you to the franchisor in advance, so you may get a more attentive interaction at the outset.

The introduction call allows you to get a clear overview of the franchise concept. The franchise rep may have an introduction prepared for you; he or she will answer your questions; and the rep will take the opportunity to get to know you. In many ways, this call is like an interview—a mutual interview—or even like a first date. So be sure you're on time and on your game. The franchisor rep will want to know if you would be a good franchisee. You want to know if the company would make a good partner—one you could trust with your life savings. There's a lot on the line for everyone involved.

The introduction call or webinar may well be your first person-to-person interaction with the franchisor, and as such it can give you your first real insight into the culture, vibe, or personality of the company you're dealing with. Occasionally, a candidate will come away from that first call thinking, "I'm not sure I can relate to these people," and sometimes the opposite happens—a connection strengthens the candidate's interest in investing.

Recently, one of my own candidates called me and confessed he'd cried when he went to tell his wife about the call. Why the tears? Because his conversation the CEO of his first-choice franchise marked the first time this candidate felt certain he was making the right decision. He had found his perfect match, and his relief was overwhelming.

INVESTIGATION STEP TWO:
FRANCHISE DISCLOSURE DOCUMENT

The second big step in franchise investigation is receiving and reviewing the franchise disclosure document (or FDD). In most cases, after your introductory call, the franchisor will offer to send it to you, and you'll likely agree.

The Federal Trade Commission requires all franchises to have an FDD in place and to provide it to potential investors before any contracts are signed or money changes hands. The FDD is written by attorneys to follow a very specific and regimented format, addressing each of twenty-three separate items. It can range from a few dozen pages to a few hundred pages of legalese, so if you have trouble sleeping at night, it might give you some relief.

Despite being tedious, though, the FDD is an invaluable tool to protect both franchisors and franchisees. This document provides a detailed portrait of the company you're considering investing your hard-earned dollars with. Whereas the introductory call might allow you to get a better sense of the human side of the company you're interested in, the FDD shares nuts and bolts information about who runs the company, what kind of background it has, and how it operates. It clearly defines and details the relationship between franchisor and franchisee, spelling out the obligations of each party. The FDD allows a potential franchisee to make an informed business decision with all the facts in hand.

Some candidates find the FDD too dense and technical to follow and may want an attorney who specializes in franchising to help them understand it. Whether you ask a franchise attorney to interpret the FDD or choose to manage it on your own, having a basic understanding of what each numbered section of the document is expected to cover and what kinds of issues you might want to be on the lookout for can help make sense of it.

What follows is a list of each item and a short explanation to help give you some perspective on this resource. Keep in mind that the opportunity to ask questions comes part and parcel with receipt of the FDD, and the franchisor should be willing to schedule a Q&A after you read. If you need clarification, be sure to follow up with questions.

Item 1: Company Background

Contains: The name and some history of the franchising company, including disclosure of any parent, predecessor, and affiliate companies.

What to Look For: Is this a new company? Is it a reincarnation of a previously failed company? Or an affiliate of a troubled corporation? Does it have a parent or affiliate companies with a track record of success?

Item 2: Franchisor Leadership

Contains: A list of the key players in the franchising company and a short professional biography for each.

What to Look For: Read this section with an eye toward understanding the levels of experience and success the primary players have not just in their field, but also in franchising. Success in an industry doesn't necessarily equate to success in franchising. It's always nice to see both.

Items 3 and 4: Litigation and Bankruptcies

Contains: The franchisor discloses in these sections if the company or any of the principals are involved in active or pending litigation or bankruptcy proceedings. These items may include claims filed *by* or *against* the franchisor.

What to Look For: In an ideal world, a franchisor would have nothing to report in either of these sections, but in practice, litigation is a reality that is sometimes unavoidable—especially when you're dealing with a large corporation. Be wary, though, if you see a pattern of lawsuits filed by franchisees.

Items 5–7: Fees and Initial Investment Estimate

Contains: Item 5 lists initial fees for buying the franchise; these are largely up-front and one-time costs. Item 6 lists additional and ongoing fees for franchise ownership. Item 7 estimates the expense to open and operate a franchise outlet for the first three months of business.

What to Look For: By the time you receive the FDD, you will probably have a good understanding of the initial fees for the franchise in question, but the breakdown of long-term fees in Item 6 may be your first clear and detailed view of how the franchisor makes money from each unit in the long run. Be sure you have an understanding of the royalty rates, advertising fees, training and consulting fees, and other expenses to which the franchisor will be entitled.

In the case of Item 7, the numbers provided will offer an invaluable glimpse into the total costs of opening a franchise unit. That said, be mindful of the numbers that are *not* on this page. The franchisor's calculation doesn't factor in investor costs that lie outside the scope of the FDD. Among those are your living and other personal expenses during the start-up period. Also left unmentioned is the fact that many start-ups take several months to break even—and so you must be sufficiently capitalized to operate until the business begins paying for itself.

Undercapitalization is the biggest potential threat to any start-up, and so you need to do your own math—preferably with the help of a trusted accountant—to predict your costs during those first few critical months. Develop a robust business pro forma and use it as your guide.

> *If you reach the FDD stage with multiple franchise companies, I recommend making a simple chart to directly compare as many of the Item 5, 6, and 7 figures as possible. This will help you gain a little perspective on what each of your investment possibilities would cost.*

Item 8: Restrictions on Sources of Products and Services

Contains: In order to provide consistent products and services, companies often require franchisees to buy supplies, equipment, software, etc., through their corporate channels. This section details what you will have to buy through your franchisor.

What to Look For: It's not uncommon for the franchisor to make a profit margin through supply sales. In an ideal system, though, the franchisor's bulk purchasing power will still offer the franchisee savings over what he or she would pay for these products in the open market. Make a note to ask actual franchisees about the fairness of their product and service costs in your next investigation step.

Item 9: Franchisee's Obligations

Contains: A list of all the franchisee's responsibilities to the franchisor, each cross-referenced to its appropriate section in the FDD.

What to Look For: Despite being labeled Item 9, this section of the FDD serves as the organizational center of the whole document. Use this section to review your obligations and to make a list of any questions or concerns about each. Item 9 can be very helpful in figuring out which areas of the FDD are unclear to you and might require further explanation.

Item 10: Financing

Contains: Disclosure if the franchisor offers any financing to new franchisees, or if it has established relationships with outside lenders to help franchisees borrow funds.

What to Look For: Consider any franchisor financing options alongside all of your other options, comparing rates and terms with equal weight.

Item 11: Franchisor's Assistance, Advertising, Computer Systems and Training

Contains: A summary of franchisor support systems for its franchisees.

What to Look For: You want to see a detailed, well-thought-out system of franchisee support under this heading. In the last chapter, you were trying to get a sense of these business systems through research and experience with established units. This is your chance to see the actual components of the system.

Beyond brand recognition, the processes and steps outlined in this section represent a large part of what you're paying for when you invest. How much and what kind of training will be provided? Will the franchisor send someone to help onsite at your opening? What kind of advertising will your investment buy? Look for a thorough and supportive system, and be alert to any qualifying language like "*up to* X hours training" or "X hours training *if deemed necessary.*" Item 11 should give you confidence the franchisor will support you throughout your partnership.

Item 12: Territory

Contains: A summary of the franchisor's territory protections for your investment.

What to Look For: After reading this section, you should feel assured that another XYZ franchise won't be opening up a block away from your retail unit, nor will another start catering to the territory of your service unit.

Items 13 and 14: Trademarks, Patents, Copyrights, and Proprietary Information

Contains: These items are self-explanatory disclosure of proprietary protections.

Item 15: Obligation to Participate

Contains: This item simply clarifies if the franchisee is required to personally manage the unit or if this can be hired out.

What to Look For: Chances are, you would not have gotten this far in the process if the company's requirements did not match your goals.

Item 16: Restrictions on Sales

Contains: Clarification of what the franchisee can and cannot offer for sale under the franchising agreement.

What to Look For: This section should be fairly straightforward— after all, part of the appeal of buying a franchise is knowing you'll be distributing a reliable product using a uniform system.

Item 17: Renewal, Termination, Transfer and Dispute Resolution

Contains: This item will be presented as a chart and, in addition to defining the basic terms of agreement, it will cover almost every "what if" scenario you can imagine. What if you decide to sell the franchise? What if you break their rules and they want to take it from you? What if you want to sell? What if they go into bankruptcy?

What to Look For: Keep in mind that when you invest in a franchise you are not, per se, "buying" it. You are buying the rights to use the name, image, and systems of the franchise for a set period of time. A typical agreement might be for ten years with first right of refusal if you decide to renew. Be sure you understand this section and what you are getting—most of us have learned just how fast ten years can fly by. You want to know what your position will be at the end of your initial investment.

Item 18: Public Figures

Contains: This section only pertains to a tiny portion of franchise investors.

Item 19: Financial Performance Representations

Contains: Item 19 can be an especially valuable section of the FDD—*if* the franchisor includes any information for you to review there. Disclosure of facts and figures in this section is voluntary, and so in many FDDs all you'll find under Item 19 is a note declining to disclose. *What to Look For:* Don't dismiss a franchisor for not providing this information in the FDD—more than half of them don't do so. However, if you *do* receive a detailed Item 19 section, consider it an excellent opportunity to grasp the most elusive financial information in franchising. Franchisors have some freedom to choose which information is presented here—like averages or top performers or the numbers from a sample of five units—but they do have to present only facts and explain where the information comes from. I love to see an Item 19 on an FDD—it offers a window into financial information you'll otherwise only have access to if you're able to talk an existing franchisee into sharing it.

Item 20: Outlets and Franchisee Information

Contains: Tables outlining the number of franchises, number of franchise transfers, and number of anticipated new franchises in a three-year period. List of current and former franchisees.

What to Look For: This section should show a trend of stability or steady growth. Obviously, you don't want to see a chart indicating a large numbers of transfers or closures. The list of franchisees is gold. You will use it to choose and reach out to a cross-section of franchisees in the next investigation step. They are your best source of good information about the viability of your investment.

Item 21: Financial Statements

Contains: Audited financial statements from the franchisor (not from franchisees).

What to Look For: One thing any candidate wants to see in a franchisor is financial stability. Is this company healthy and does it have cash to invest or use to ride out stormy times? Another key element to identify in Item 21 is how the franchisor makes money. Occasionally, a franchisor gets along by bootstrapping, sustaining itself on franchise fees rather than royalties coming in from successful franchisees. This business model will inevitably fall apart in the long run—and you don't want to be a part of that. Look for solid financials driven by royalties and fees coming in from franchisees.

Items 22 and 23: Contracts and Receipts

Contains: Franchisee contracts for your review and receipt acknowledging you have been given the Franchise Disclosure Document.

What to Look For: For now, these items are just formalities. Save them for your records and possible future review.

> *I love to see an Item 19 on a Financial Disclosure Document—it offers a window into financial information you'll otherwise only have access to if you're able to talk an existing franchisee into sharing it.*

DON'T MAKE THIS MISTAKE:
INVESTING WITH AN INEXPERIENCED LEADERSHIP TEAM

Now that you've seen the FDD, you have some insight into the professional backgrounds of each franchisor's leadership team. Don't choose an unproven, untested team. Ask any business executive about his or her biggest mistakes, and you'll hear some doozies. Each of those mistakes was made in some previous year or with some previous company. Don't choose a team that has yet to make its big mistakes! As you review those corporate bios, ask yourself, "Does this leadership team have the know-how and business acumen to take the franchisor to the next level?"

If the answer to that question is yes, then ask one more: "Is this team great at franchising—or are they great at something else and just getting their feet wet as a franchise?" There's a big difference between being proficient at running an individual business and having the experience required to roll that idea into a large, repeatable franchise concept. Possession of a great idea or one finely tuned business is a wonderful thing, but it's only a small component in the building of a successful franchise.

INVESTIGATION STEP THREE:
VALIDATION CALLS

Validation calls are your chance to speak with real, live franchisees, people who have already been down the path you're looking at and wondering about. There's no better way to get the feedback you need to make an informed decision than by getting in the trenches and talking with those who have gone before you. Talking to franchisees, you get the opportunity to ask the good, the bad, and the ugly questions—and usually to get direct answers.

Each franchise company has a slightly different process when it comes to making validation calls, but the franchisor is not a part of these conversations. Some franchise companies will provide a list of franchisees that are more than willing to take the time to share information with you; these will be good validator of whatever the franchisor has told you already. There are other franchise companies whose franchisees are so busy and inundated with calls from prospective investors that there's no way that they can get back to everybody. In those circumstances, franchise companies will sometimes do group validation calls, where there'll be a franchisee or two on a call with several prospective franchisees asking questions and hearing all the answers. While this is an efficient way to provide information, it doesn't allow you to ask the kinds of more probing questions about the individual's experience that might really enlighten you.

And that's why you should, in addition to participating in whatever calls the franchisor helps set up, go out on your own. Every FDD includes a list of franchisees. You may make contact on your own initiative with these people for validation calls. It's up to them, of course, whether or not they return your call, but if you are polite and persistent, you should be able to get valuable responses.

When making validation calls, it's a good idea to go for a mix of people who've been in the system for varying lengths of time: one year, five years, ten years; as well as people who've had varying degrees of success. Tapping a good, representative cross-section of franchisees is very important—you want as complete and honest an understanding of the franchisor as you can possibly get.

How do you make the most of this opportunity? First, remember that the franchisee has no obligation to speak with you or to share private information about how his or her business runs. Most franchisees do this as a courtesy because someone else did it for them—they understand that this step is crucial for any investor and know how much their input can mean to a candidate. Since the franchisees are in essence volunteers sharing their time and experience, be considerate and appreciative of their time.

Start your call with an easy ice-breaker question to make a connection and show your interest. I find most people respond well when you ask how they came to own a particular franchise— and their answers are often very informative for a potential owner.

Next, move on to questions that carry a little more weight. You definitely want to ask about corporate training—what it is;

how it is; what its shortcomings are. If appropriate, inquire about how the franchisor assisted with site selection and if the franchisee was happy with the process. Ask about marketing support and the use of advertising dollars. Does the franchisee feel he or she is getting a good return on marketing investment?

When you've covered these non-intrusive topics and any others you'd like to pursue—like staffing and corporate support—then go ahead and ask the questions the franchisee knows are coming. These are the questions about revenues, profit margins, time to breakeven—all the money questions your mother told you to never ask. Be polite and clear about what you want to know. Remember that the franchisee was likely on your end of many of these calls not so long ago, and he or she knows you need this information to make a good decision. Be sure to thank the franchisees for their time and the information they've shared with you. Also, at the end of the call, ask for permission to circle back if you have any more questions.

Not everyone will answer every question, but in my experience, these calls are the key to really seeing behind the curtain and into how the franchise system is working for people like you.

> *Validation calls are your chance to speak with real, live franchisees, people who have already been down the path you're looking at and wondering about.*

INVESTIGATION STEP FOUR:
DISCOVERY DAY

The last core investigation step is the discovery day or meet-the-team day. Once you've narrowed down your choices, visiting a franchise headquarters can be a great way to get a feel for whether a franchise is a fit for you. Keep in mind the goals of a site visit for a franchise company are to sell you on their concept and to get to know you. In some cases, this may be the step at which *they* decide whether or not to approve *you*, and the point at which you make your final decision as to whether you want to be a part of their business.

When you do a discovery day, you may get to visit the corporate headquarters, meet the leadership team, meet the support team, and see operations. Some companies don't do this kind of thing, but instead may send a senior member of the franchise team to visit you and evaluate you. Some even conduct online discovery days. In my experience, this step is a great opportunity to gather that last intel you need to make an informed choice, so if the company you're looking at offers a discovery experience, I recommend it wholeheartedly.

Everybody does discovery a little bit differently, but one thing is true across the board. This is the franchisor's show. Regardless of what they show you or how you spend your visit, you will learn a lot about how the company operates and how it treats its franchisees.

If you have a spouse or a business partner, discovery day is something you should do together. It's a very important step—usually the very last before you either sign on the dotted line or decide to take a pass. Consider it your final inspection—you're there not to research so much as to confirm.

So how will you spend your discovery day? Every program varies, but these are some of the ways your time can be best used:

Get to Know the Boss. In almost every case, discovery day is your opportunity to get to know the franchise's leadership team. You'll get to shake their hands and look them in the eyes. You'll be asking yourself, "Is this a person I can trust to invest my dollars? To lead this business to further success?" You should be able to feel confident about both.

Meet the People Who Get Things Done. Discovery day is also your opportunity to meet the franchise's support team. This may include the person who's going to help you find real estate; the person who will teach you how the use the company's technology; the person who decides how to spend your pooled marketing dollars; even the person who answers the phone when you dial corporate headquarters. Your interactions with these people should reassure you about the efficiency and responsiveness of the franchisor.

See the Operation in Action. When I went on a discovery day for a fitness concept, I got to try out one of the workouts. If you go to discovery for a food or retail franchise, you may well visit a working unit—perhaps one run by the corporate office. If you're looking at a gym or a spa facility, you may get to try out the services. Chances are good that whatever operation you visit will be an exemplary performer—an example of the potential of your own investment.

When you leave a discovery day, if you haven't made a decision, you should at least have a clear sense of the character of the franchise company. The next step is a personal one: your own decision day.

DON'T MAKE THIS MISTAKE:
THINKING YOU'RE THE ONLY PARTY
MAKING AN ASSESSMENT

It's a lesser-known fact of this kind of franchise investigation that franchisors are doing an investigation of their own. As you interact with them, they will weigh your strengths and weaknesses alongside those of other potential franchisees to choose the best match for their goals. Some franchise openings are quite competitive, and many franchisors are not afraid to turn away potential buyers who don't seem like a good fit for their image. Just remember throughout the process that you aren't shopping for an investment—you're looking for a win/win relationship—and that's what the franchisor is looking for, too.

═══ SUCCESS STORY: ═══
BREAKING THE EXECUTIVE MOLD WITH SELF-INVESTMENT

Background: Rick was a consumer-marketing director for a major retailer when he and four hundred of his co-workers were laid off. While sitting in the waiting room at an executive transition company, he read an article about executive coaching in *Entrepreneur* and thought that could be the path for him.

Search Process: Rick worked with a franchise consultant to explore a number of different types of investment opportunities, but in the end, his skills and goals matched his initial inspiration and seemed best suited to executive coaching.

Decision: Rick bought a business-coaching franchise. He chose a franchise over starting his own business because he wanted a ready-made and detailed process for getting up and running. "Lots of smart people want to go out on their own," he says, "but I wanted to know how to build something profitable and predictable."

Result: There are several stages of being a start-up business: obtaining your first clients, achieving breakeven, making decent money, and then, for Rick, replacing your corporate income. Rick is now in that ultimate phase, making more money than he did in his corporate position, and enjoying more flexibility. "I don't worry whether I will get promoted, or whether someone else will, or if I will be shipped to a new area," Rick says. "And I'm making a difference in more people's lives. People hire me for my ability to drive their businesses. Hearing, 'That's a great idea,' and, 'Thank you,' never gets old."

Best Advice: "I think the challenge for executives is that we're not used to investing our own money in ourselves," Rick says. "That's one of the reasons I have such a profound respect for business owners; they're making bets on themselves, on their employees, on marketing actions and other important business investments every day. When you're initially looking at putting up the money—in my case, it was over $100,000—in a sense, it feels like you're buying a job. You need to pivot your thinking to the mindset of making an investment. In this case you are investing in yourself and your family. That requires a different way of looking at things than anything in my corporate experience."

CHAPTER SUMMARY

- When you've narrowed your franchise options down to just three or four, it's time to go through the process of franchise investigation for all of them—to the end or until an option no longer seems viable.

- The four main steps of franchise investigation are the introductory call, receipt of the Franchise Disclosure Document, validation calls, and discovery day.

- Validation calls are your very best opportunity to peek behind the curtain at a franchisor's inner workings. Be sure you make the most of this opportunity.

- Each of these steps will give you a new depth of knowledge and understanding of the franchise company. By the end of the process, you should feel confident in making a decision about investing in one of your three investment prospects.

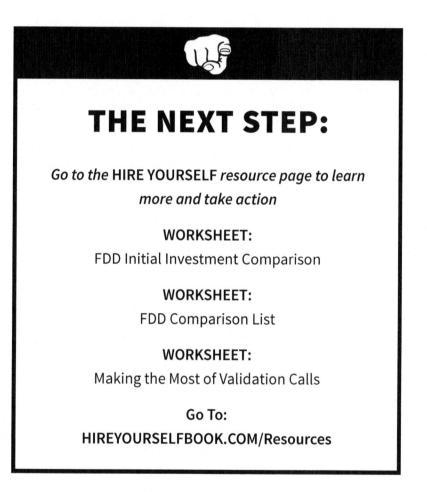

THE NEXT STEP:

Go to the **HIRE YOURSELF** *resource page to learn more and take action*

WORKSHEET:

FDD Initial Investment Comparison

WORKSHEET:

FDD Comparison List

WORKSHEET:

Making the Most of Validation Calls

Go To:

HIREYOURSELFBOOK.COM/Resources

PART III

REAL STEPS TOWARD REAL SUCCESS

CHAPTER 7

CAN YOU AFFORD IT? CAPITALIZING YOUR INVESTMENT

"Capital isn't scarce; vision is."

—SAM WALTON

s an investor, I've been on the buying side of the franchise equation, and I know just how it feels to make the huge leap from thinking about a business to actually signing over a chunk of your precious savings for it. As an executive, I was making a six-figure salary— one that covered the costs of my family's home, cars, food—even vacations and dance lessons. When I bought the rights to a junk-removal franchise, I walked away from that corporate salary with the understanding that I would not have any income for the immediate future.

Not knowing just how long it'll take before your business starts cash flowing is one of the toughest challenges of going out on your own. That kind of risk doesn't come easily to anyone, and it requires a certain amount of hope and faith. Before you move forward on optimism, though, you must make an honest assessment of your assets, develop a clear understanding of what you'll need to bring to your deal and just how much risk you'll assume, and decide how you'll assemble the necessary investment through a combination of liquid capital and loans.

GET YOUR FINANCIAL DUCKS IN A ROW

The leap from *investigating* a franchise to *buying* one requires a reality check from any potential investor. Are you sure you can put together the necessary capital to buy into the concept you've chosen? Do you feel confident your choice is a good risk? Can you overcome your natural anxiety about change and chances to make the investment?

As you answer these questions and investigate the options available for capitalizing, you should be able to have increasing confidence in the feasibility of your plan. I had every reason to feel positive and hopeful when I bought into that first franchise, and I try to help each candidate I work with commit to his or her investment with the kind of assurance that comes from knowing due diligence has been done and the odds are stacked for success.

There are three main components that will determine your investment threshold, and two of these will eventually make up your capitalization: your net worth, your liquid capital, and your available financing.

Net Worth

Let's talk about your net worth first. Before you commit to any franchise concept, you need to know your documentable net worth. Every franchisor and every lender will have some measure of net worth they want you to meet as an assurance that you are financially solvent enough to successfully launch a new business.

To calculate your net worth, start with a summary of your assets, and then subtract your liabilities. Don't forget to include investment and retirement accounts, annuities, and any loans in your name. Your calculations should look something like this:

QUICK NET WORTH CALCULATION

FIRST, *ADD* UP THE VALUE OF YOUR ASSETS:

- _____ CASH (Including checking, savings, money market accounts)
- _____ INVESTMENTS (Including stocks, bonds, CDs, annuities, mutual funds)
- _____ RETIREMENT FUNDS (Including 401ks, IRAs, other pension plans)
- _____ PROPERTY HOLDINGS (Market value of high-value possessions, including real estate, cars, boats, etc.)

= _____ *TOTAL ASSETS*

NEXT, *ADD* UP THE VALUE OF YOUR LIABILITIES:

- _____ MORTGAGE DEBT (Include second mortgages or exercised lines of credit)
- _____ OTHER LOANS (Include auto loans, student loans, personal loans, etc.)
- _____ CURRENT DEBTS (Include credit card, legal, medical, and other debts)

= _____ *TOTAL LIABILITIES*

NOW, *SUBTRACT* YOUR LIABILITIES FROM YOUR TOTAL ASSETS

- _____ TOTAL ASSETS
- _____ TOTAL LIABILITIES

= _____ *YOUR NET WORTH*

If you have a very low or negative net worth number, you probably need to wait and beef up the asset side of your balance sheet (or reduce the debt side) before you move forward with franchise investment. Most franchisors have a specific range of minimum net worth in mind for their franchisees, and that number is usually based on their experiences with successful (and sometimes unsuccessful) launches. They want to know you are financially sound enough to withstand the test of becoming a business owner.

Liquid Capital

If your net worth is within the recommended range that your franchise consultant or the franchise you have in mind suggest, your next step is assessing your liquid capital. This is the money you could, if you had to, produce in cash or easily convert to cash. Your liquid capital includes funds in savings accounts and accessible stock investments. As a guideline, you can expect to need a minimum of $50,000 to $100,000 of available liquid capital for a service-based franchise concept and a minimum of $75,000 to $100,000 for a facility-based franchise. Depending on the size of the commitment you make with your franchise agreement—for instance, in the case of a multiple territory development schedule or an exceptionally large and costly facility—you might need substantially more money at the table. Keep in mind that these numbers only represent your *liquid* capital investment—not your *total* investment. Your total investment will include the liquid assets you commit to your project along with the financing you secure.

Your total available liquid capital may not all be sitting in a savings account or accessible at the ATM. If you don't have sufficient liquid assets in savings to reach the investment threshold for your franchise of choice, you may have *convertible assets* that can add to your total. Home equity is one example. If your home is worth more than you own on your mortgage, you may be able to access that value through a line of credit, thus converting it to a liquid asset. Retirement savings can also sometimes be leveraged to support your franchise investment through accounts that allow for self-directed investments. We'll talk more about the advantages and drawbacks of this kind of account later in this chapter. The main point here is that if you have built up equity through your real estate or retirement investments, you may be able to tap that equity to create liquid capital. Doing so is a very personal decision and one that should not be taken lightly. I have worked with candidates who've leveraged these assets to great advantage, but I recommend each investor carefully weigh the risks of tapping into this kind of resource.

However you assemble the funds, your liquid capital serves two main purposes. The first is obvious: it helps pay for your initial investment, augmenting your loans and any other finance arrangements. Second, your liquid capital represents your "skin in the game," as the saying goes. When you put up as much as $100,000 of your own money to buy into a franchise concept, you demonstrate a tremendous personal commitment to the success of that investment. The franchisor wants you to be that committed, and so do the lenders who help you access the balance of your startup capital.

Credit History

Your credit history is a less tangible, but very important, part of your financial self-assessment. If you've made a habit of keeping your financial house in order, you'll be rewarded when franchisors start looking at your suitability for their brand. Franchisors may consider your credit rating, your proven financial stability, your tenure as an employee in various positions, and your payment histories when they weigh the risks of granting you a franchise. As part of your own due diligence, order a copy of your credit report and look for any inconsistencies or concerns. You'll need to be prepared to explain any issues you find there.

ASSESS YOUR RISK TOLERANCE

We've all heard of people who put their last dollar on the line to start a business. FedEx founder Fred Smith, for example, famously played blackjack with his last cash on hand to make payroll for his fledgling company. Others have leveraged houses, family heirlooms, and their last dimes to buy into a great concept. For most of us, though, the idea of risking everything ranks right up there with parasailing in a thunderstorm or drag racing in the family car. You've worked hard for your assets, and you need to find a level of investment that fits your comfort level for risk. Somewhere between clinging to the same paycheck every other week (or doggedly job seeking to replace it) and putting everything you've worked for on the line is a range in which each investor can find a manageable risk level.

Once you've calculated the value of your assets, it's time to ask yourself how much of those assets you're comfortable to leverage for investment. I don't recommend investing more than 50 percent to 75 percent of your cash reserves, and when possible, I'd suggest holding onto as much cash as possible. The phrase "keep your powder dry" is a smart principle when capitalizing your business. Having extra cash available is always a good thing. Over time, if you don't need that cash, in most cases you can pay off loans or other funding sources early. Until then, it's important to have a personal reserve, and a business one as well.

Two factors that should be critical in determining how much cash you keep on hand are your projected business operating costs and the anticipated living expenses you don't have covered by another source of income until you've crossed the breakeven point with your business. You must expect to have a negative cash flow for a while. Calculate your average monthly outflows, and always err on the side of caution when determining how long you might need to pay those debts from savings or from a salary you build into your business expenses. Your validation calls with existing franchisees provide you with a good idea of how long you might wait before seeing a positive cash flow. Until then, your best move is to leverage as much capital as possible through loans so you've got the reserves to take care of yourself and your family.

> *Unless you have unlimited cash reserves, a good guideline is to invest no more than 50 percent to 75 percent of your cash in a business.*

THE BUSINESS OF BORROWING STARTS WITH A PLAN

No matter who you approach or where you decide to seek funding for your investment, you'll be better prepared to make a case and negotiate the best possible terms if you've done your homework in advance. Putting together a solid business plan before you file any applications or sit down with a finance company, a loan officer—even with a family member—will help you make a clear, compelling case.

You've undoubtedly heard the saying, "Failing to plan is planning to fail," and in no sphere is that more true than in starting a business. If you've never developed a business plan, hire somebody to help you. A solidly prepared plan will not only help you secure financing, but it will also serve as a guidepost as you build your business in the months and years to come. When you feel organized and confident in your plan, you'll be ready to put it to work for you in borrowing from others.

Your business plan should include each of these basic components:

Executive Summary

Picture this: You've found the perfect franchise concept. You're uniquely positioned to run it. You've got a great location in mind, stellar employees waiting in the wings, and a substantial percentage of the required investment sitting in the bank waiting to be pressed into service. You go to a business conference and win the biggest door prize imaginable: a three-minute pitch session with Warren Buffett himself. What would you say to convince one of the wisest businessmen in American history to invest in your franchise?

Whatever you'd use your three minutes for—that's what belongs in the Executive Summary of your business plan. This is your pitch page—your big chance to explain (1) what need your business will fill, (2) why the business you're planning is a brilliant way to meet that need, and (3) why you are the best possible person to bring that business to success.

You'd be wise to work on the assumption that the executive summary is the *only* part of your proposal a potential investor or lender will read. If it doesn't make a strong case for turning the page, it will be.

Ideally, your executive summary should be accessible and professional, and should highlight the unique need for the business you propose. The concept of the franchise you have in mind is your best ally here—if the franchise has taken off like gangbusters in California, for example, and you're getting in on the ground floor in Colorado, you can offer a proven history of success. Whatever it is that distinguishes the concept—something that's already been well and thoroughly tested by the franchisor—that works in your favor, as well. Great placement, a unique service or customer treatment, a marketing edge, an innovative product— all these things make your summary stand out.

When it comes to your own qualifications, this is the moment to boast. Did you run a billion-dollar department for your previous employer? Has your experience given you unique access to the industry or community? Are you enthusiastic, committed, and uniquely able to run this business? Tell Mr. Buffett (or rather, the readers of your Executive Summary) *why* on your first page, while you've got their attention. Keep your information clear, focused and at the macro level. If you write a great summary, your reader will go deeper into your plan to find the specifics.

Like a great resume or book pitch, a strong executive summary for a new business should be kept to one or two pages at most.

Business Description

What kind of business is it that you're changing your life to launch? What need does it fill? What are the products and services it will offer? Who will it serve? Why will it have a competitive advantage? Your franchisor should have already answered all of these questions for you, and so your job in terms of the Business Proposal is to share those answers and customize them to the specific unit or units you intend to launch.

Industry Outlook/Competitive Analysis

Your industry outlook should briefly summarize the history of the industry you seek to break into and offer a realistic and enthusiastic snapshot of potential/expected growth. Explain why this growth is coming (for example: a growing demographic or an up-and-coming trend) and how your company will be uniquely positioned to meet the need. This section should feature hard numbers and well-researched projections—a great place for graphs or demographics. These are components your franchisor may be able to provide.

Your competitive analysis should identify the competitors your business will face and lay out the strengths and weaknesses of each. This is your opportunity to point out an unmet need or unique point of entry into the market.

Marketing and Sales Information

What is your strategy for bringing customers to your business—or bringing your business to them? How will you build a customer base and how will you keep that base growing? What sales strategies will drive your success? Your franchisor will have already not only researched, but also successfully implemented these strategies. The same reasons you find the company a compelling investment should be the reasons your lender or investor is willing to put money behind it, too.

Operations and Management

How will you run your business? What are the logistical challenges, and what are the solutions you're ready to implement? What will your daily tasks and responsibilities entail? What about those of your employees? How many employees will work for you? This is the section that should include the nitty-gritty details of how you will run your operation. Being able to articulate them here demonstrates to the lender that you've thought things through to the last detail.

Financial Data

This section will include a clear depiction of how much money it will take to make your business fully operational and where that funding will come from. Your franchisor and its Franchise Disclosure Document will be a good source of information about the startup and operating costs of the business. As with all sections of the business plan, pitching a franchise means you have far less guesswork to do than you would if you were launching an unknown entity.

Sample Financial Pro Forma

A pro forma is a projection of a business's future costs, sales, and other financials based on the information available. You can find sample pro formas online, but you may need the help of an accountant to create a feasible projection for this portion of your business plan. Also the franchisor may be able to provide a blank pro forma that is specific for their business model. No one has a crystal ball when it comes to the financial future, but as a potential franchisee, you should be able to create a well-thought-out estimate of expected expenses and sales. Keep in mind that a pro forma is a living document that you will adjust and tweak as you move forward with the business. Like a battle plan, the pro forma is going to change once you engage, but the process of putting it together is invaluable in terms of giving you an understanding of both the certainties and the possibilities.

Keep in mind as you are pulling together your financing plan that any type of debt equity you take on will have to be paid back in regular installments off the top of your cash flow from the new business. Incorporate your debt service payment into your financial pro forma.

> *You've undoubtedly heard the saying, "Failing to plan is planning to fail," and in no sphere is that more true than in starting a business. If you've never developed a business plan, hire somebody to help you. A solidly prepared plan will not only help you secure financing, but it will also serve as a guidepost as you build your business in the months and years to come.*

DON'T MAKE THIS MISTAKE: GOING INTO BUSINESS UNDERCAPITALIZED

The biggest known danger to any new business is undercapitalization. You can't give your investment a chance to take root and grow if you aren't prepared to nurture it and wait for it to thrive. Make sure you have a good understanding of all the startup and ongoing expenses so you have plenty of capital to tide you over through the early stages of your launch. We've all heard stories about the guy that started a business on a shoestring and then made millions. What you don't hear is all the stuff that happened to get him from here to there. Or about all the other entrepreneurs who didn't make it when they took the same approach. Bootstrapping is not a viable long-term business model. You need cash flow to make the transition from startup to success.

SMART, SAVVY BORROWING: WHOM TO ASK AND HOW

With your business plan in hand, it's time to tap all your available resources to find the best available financing at the lowest possible cost to you. As you enter this phase of capitalization, keep in mind that there are lenders, accountants, and attorneys who specialize in franchise financing. We'll talk a little more about these individuals in the coming section, but in some cases, they represent your best chance of a smooth, successful financing experience.

At this point in the process of buying a franchise, you may want to meet with a funding specialist. This consultant can help you explore and execute the best funding strategies for your business. Whether you work with a consultant or strike out on your own, I recommend starting your financing investigations by weighing your ability and willingness to leverage your own assets and working your way from there to conventional and other potential lending sources.

Home Equity

If you are a homeowner, you may be able to leverage the equity you have in your home through a home equity line of credit (HELOC), or a home equity loan (HEL). There are advantages and disadvantages associated with utilizing the equity in your home to help capitalize a business. The biggest advantage, of course, is that you are leveraging your own existing equity and should be able to do so at a relatively low interest rate. The disadvantage is the inherent risk involved in putting your home up as collateral for your business. Use caution and be sure you don't assume more risk than you could handle if your business runs into trouble.

Retirement Funds

You can also leverage retirement funds for your business investment by utilizing retirement savings, 401(k) savings or IRAs. To avoid penalties, you can work with a company that specializes in helping investors take advantage of the Entrepreneur Rollover Stock Ownership Plan (ERSOP) or Rollovers as Business Startups (ROBS) plan to fund new businesses. In these scenarios, your retirement funds become the "investor" in your business. Instead of those funds being invested in publically traded equities or fixed-income investments, your retirement account owns stock in your corporation. Using this kind of account is more complicated than this simple analogy might make it seem, so make sure you work with a reputable investment professional to ensure your ERSOP or ROBS is set up and executed correctly. It will be a costly mistake if it's done incorrectly.

As with the use of home equity funds in business investment, use caution as you look at utilizing your retirement dollars. You've saved that money to provide yourself with long-term security, and there are risks involved in putting it on the line for a business venture. There are also, as we all know, risks involved in investing in the stock market, as traditional retirement funds do. My point is simply that you must be aware of how much risk you're taking and what your plan will be if that risk does not pay off.

Family and Friends

Gifts, loans, and investments from family members can be a great source of capital for your business. I worked with one candidate who ended up recruiting both his father and brother in his investment, and they successfully launched multiple units of a franchise they all hope to profit from for some time to come.

If you do accept funds from people you have personal relationships with, make sure you have an agreement in writing, with the terms and conditions of the gift, investment, or loan clearly outlined—including investment terms, payback terms, interest, and what happens if you default. Is your investor a lender or a partner? If he or she is a partner, does that mean having a say in the running of your daily operations? Having the details hammered out in an agreement may prevent a misunderstanding that could cost you a valuable relationship with a family member or a friend. Situations involving family and pooled money always have the potential to get sticky, so make sure everyone understands the risks and, again, put it all in writing.

Franchisor (or franchisor-assisted) financing

Another source of financing is franchisor financing, which can be via direct assistance or prearranged third party financing by the franchisor. Not all franchisors offer it, and programs may vary widely. Some may not require collateral, or might offer equipment leasing. Some offer deferred payments. Some may have low-interest rates, but some may not even be competitive with traditional loans. Check with your franchisor to see what programs they may offer before branching out to explore your other options. Then be sure to compare all the choices available to you.

Franchise Financing Companies

There are some companies that specialize in financing franchise businesses and can offer assistance with figuring out how to capitalize yours. These companies understand the franchise business model and have relationships with financial institutions that fund franchise loans. Some also specialize in assisting clients with utilizing retirement funds as ROBS (Rollovers as Business Startups plans) and in securing U.S. Small Business Administration loans.

In many cases, these companies may have preapproved dollars set aside for helping people invest in franchised businesses. For example, a franchisor may have a relationship with a franchise financing company in which $20 million has been pre-approved for qualified new franchisees. This can streamline the process of getting your investment dollars.

Traditional Loans

Another option is to leverage traditional business loans, or commercial loans. There are multiple types of commercial loans that can be utilized, including secured and unsecured loans, short- and long-term loans, equipment loans, and certainly business lines of credit. Expect to put up at least 20 percent of your investment to be considered for these kinds of loans, and know that many traditional lenders may not understand the franchise business model as well as lenders who specialize in this area. Still, it can sometimes be easier to get a traditional loan when buying a franchise than when investing in an unknown entity, because a proven franchise concept may look less risky to a financial institution. Additionally, your ability to get a traditional loan will depend on your personal financial health and on the business opportunity.

As with any financing source, it's always in your best interest to shop around, so make sure you check out business loans at multiple financial institutions.

U.S. Small Business Administration Loans

The SBA offers loans through participating banks and lenders, and since the SBA will guarantee up to 85 percent of the loan, there is less risk for the lender—which can translate to a lower interest rate for you. SBA financing is not really a government loan, but rather a private loan backed by government funds. There are multiple types of SBA loans you can investigate. Make sure you carefully evaluate the pros and cons associated with taking out an SBA versus a traditional loan, i.e. the cost to establish the loan, the length of the loan, and the interest rates of the loan. Note that if your franchise company is listed on the SBA registry, it may help expedite the process for a new franchisee to get an SBA loan. Also worth noting is the fact that individuals with high net worth may not qualify for this type of loan.

Other Financing Options

Online Financing Centers are online companies that serve as clearinghouses for franchise financing. These companies have multiple financial institutions in their systems to review your financial information and evaluate your request for financing. They host the equivalent of speed dating for the loan industry—you provide all of your information, then lenders review it and decide if they'd like to initiate a relationship with you. As with any lender, the onus is on you to make sure the franchising company and the lender are reputable entities. You can ask your franchise consultant to recommend an online franchise financing company with a good reputation and track record.

Angel investors or venture capitalists are private sector, wealthy individuals who might consider investing in your business. Venture capitalists are not going to invest unless they see potential for a high return. Often, you'll learn that you have to give away equity in your business as a tradeoff in this type of arrangement, so be careful to understand the terms if you are considering it. In practice, very few people actually use this method of financing; only a tiny percentage of small businesses are funded through angel investment.

DON'T MAKE THIS MISTAKE: ENTERING YOUR NEW VENTURE WITHOUT AN EXIT STRATEGY

Too many people dive into business ownership without a next step in mind. The result? They end up stuck. Simply put, you need to have a good, solid exit plan in mind, even as you assemble your capital to get the business off the ground. Great entrepreneurs always have a clear idea of what comes next. Do you plan to sell the business in five or ten years? Do you plan to transition it to a family member in the future? Knowing how you plan to dispose of your business in the long run is one key part of that vision.

SUCCESS STORY: SEEING AND SEIZING THE RIGHT OPPORTUNITY

Background: Scott always knew he wanted to own his own business one day, but when he visited a new fitness center for a free class, he fell in love with the original concept and the clean, welcoming facility in the suburbs. He set out to learn more about franchise opportunities with the same company.

Search Process: Scott started his process on the franchisor's website, and then spoke with a consultant to get a second opinion as to whether he'd make a good franchisee candidate. As he went through the franchise investigation process, Scott was impressed by the enthusiasm and competence of the franchisor's team. By the time he visited their headquarters, two months after beginning his search, he was ready to commit.

Decision: Scott wasn't positioned with a substantial amount of liquid capital to invest, but he leveraged his retirement funds and partnered with friends and family members who wanted to invest. With his capital in place, Scott invested in the fitness franchise and opened his first unit. "Of course I had a lot of anxiety about investing so much money," he says, "but I believed this was the right opportunity."

Result: With his strong background in sales, marketing, and operations, Scott is well positioned to guide his franchise investment to growth and profitability.

Best Advice: "One thing you have to be able to do well is connect with people, with your customer," Scott says, "because that's who will bring in the money. If you can't do it, you have to have somebody who can. You have to surround yourself with the people who will help you be successful by bolstering your weak points."

CHAPTER SUMMARY

- Capitalizing your investment starts with making an honest assessment of your assets so you can pinpoint your net worth and available liquid capital. Next, decide how you'll assemble the necessary investment through a combination of liquid capital and loans.

- Before you move forward with your investment, carefully consider how much risk you're willing to assume. Weigh the risks vs. benefits of tapping home equity or retirement savings for your investment. This is a personal decision that should not be influenced your franchisor or any other party involved in your investment.

- Take the time to develop a strong, detailed business plan. This tool will not only help you secure financing, but it will also serve as a guidepost as you build your business.

THE NEXT STEP:

Go to the **HIRE YOURSELF** *resource page to learn more and take action*

WORKSHEET:

Calculate Your Net Worth

WORKSHEET:

Lender Comparison

SAMPLE:

Financial Pro Forma

Go To:

HIREYOURSELFBOOK.COM/Resources

CHAPTER 8

FOUR FOUNDATIONS OF FRANCHISE SUCCESS

"A dream doesn't become reality through magic; it takes sweat, determination, and hard work."

—COLIN POWELL

hen I invested in my own business, my whole family embraced it with me. My wife is my most trusted advisor and partner, but each of my children also has a title—and a corresponding job. As the kids get older, their jobs become a little more demanding, branching out into marketing and technology. My middle daughter's current title is Motivation Chief, and she takes her role quite seriously. I often head to a meeting or the office by way of her "Good Morning, Dad. WORK HARD TODAY!" greetings and signs. And when I get home, she'll ask, "Did you hit your objectives today?"

As you launch your business, even a well-oiled franchise, you might consider enlisting a Motivation Chief (and sign-maker) of your own. You're going to want help staying motivated and moving toward your goals! As you already know, the potential rewards of owning your own business are immense, but the labor and logistics of getting that business off the ground may be the hardest work of your life. As you accomplish your goals each day, week, and month, keep sight of the fact that the person you're working for now is *you*. You—and your own contingent of partners and dependents—will reap the rewards of your labor. You've chosen your own enterprise, a win/win/win franchise concept that's been thoroughly researched and vetted, and you are more than qualified to make it a success.

In advising hundreds of franchise buyers and being one myself, I've learned a lot about orchestrating a successful launch. What follows are four of the best pieces of franchising advice I've given or received. I hope you'll find them helpful as you begin what your long and prosperous life of self-employment.

> *The potential rewards of owning your own business are immense, but the labor and logistics of getting that business off the ground may be the hardest work of your life. As you accomplish your goals each day, week, and month, keep sight of the fact that the person you're working for now is you.*

FOUNDATION #1:
LEARN THE BUSINESS

In many ways, a business is like a living entity—growing and changing all the time, especially in the beginning. In order to keep ahead of what your business is and what it's becoming, you must continually learn and grow with it. Most of the investors I work with come to franchising with a solid, often impressive knowledge of at least one aspect of running a business. Many are experienced at running large-scale and multi-faceted operations, either for corporate employers or on their own. But no matter what your professional background entails, one key to franchising success is leveraging all the training and instruction available to make your business a success.

In particular, franchisor instruction and guidance is one of the big things you paid for with your initial fee. And the best way to get your money's worth is by learning everything you can from those services. Your franchisor has a vested interest in your success, so every program they provide has the potential to be instrumental in the success and growth of your business.

Make the most of each of these learning opportunities to set yourself up for success before your launch:

Pre-Training Materials

Your franchisor will give you lots of materials to review and study prior to your training in the field or at franchise headquarters. You may receive books, videos, computer programs—or some combination of all three.

These materials are your first step in adopting the systems the franchisor has meticulously designed, so read everything, watch every video, and take it all in. Keep a running list of questions, and don't hesitate to follow up with your franchisor about anything you find unclear.

Set-Up Checklist

For many companies, new franchisees receive a checklist of things to review or accomplish prior to attending training. The items on this list vary widely from one franchise to the next and between industries, but they may include things such as leasing a facility, ordering and/or setting up equipment, and reviewing hiring guidelines. The franchisor may help you with some or all of these steps, and will provide good guidance, so don't be daunted by any of the items. Just take them one at a time.

Field or Classroom Training

This is a big blast of training, usually one or two weeks just before or just after your launch. Some franchisors invite you to come to their facility for a classroom-type environment, some come to you, and some put their own unique spin on this process. Regardless of the format, be prepared to take in a lot of information in a relatively short amount of time. You will likely spend a substantial amount of time on the operations manual—sort of the secret recipe book of the franchise. You'll also learn more about the marketing, hiring, facility setup, brand rules, and regulations—plus guidance for your successful launch.

> *The franchisor has a vested interest in your success, so every available training program has the potential to be instrumental in the success and growth of your business.*

Franchisor-Approved Third-Party Players

Your franchise company may have outside vendors that understand the business and can help optimize your preparations. These companies are chosen by the franchisor because they have a unique understanding and mastery of what it takes for your particular franchise to succeed.

Among the frequently utilized third-party players are real estate companies that can help you identify an ideal facility or location and negotiate a lease, developers who can build out your property to the franchisor's specs and handle everything from blueprints to permits to post-build inspections, marketing companies with proprietary expertise specific to your franchisor, and technical consultants who can help set your systems up to efficiently utilize the prescribed technology.

Your franchisor has developed a relationship with these companies and their representatives will know the program backward and forward. Working hand in hand with them can make your ramp-up experience much easier.

Your Own Trusted Advisors

Whether or not you're new to the business of franchise ownership, there will be times when you're faced with decisions that seem beyond your expertise. At those times, you need people you can trust to steer you in the right direction.

Fortunately, investing in franchising comes with some great built-in advisors—including your franchise consultant, your franchisor's team, and your fellow franchisees. In addition, you may choose to seek advice from an accountant, bookkeeper, business coach, or franchise attorney from time to time.

No matter who you turn to for referrals or advice, don't forget to pay attention to your inner Jiminy Cricket. If someone doesn't click with you, or if the advice you're hearing doesn't ring right, get a reality check in the form of an objective second opinion.

You may find the objectivity you need among your own trusted advisors—that teacher, parent, business coach, or professional mentor who's never led you astray. As I look back on my own career, the guidance of my trusted advisors plays a significant role. My mentor Wes Kimes gave me the courage to seriously consider entrepreneurship. Darren Hardy, first through his books and later through personal mentoring, helped me become more effective in my business and personal life and encouraged me to write a book of my own. Anthony Robbins, through his seminars and the once-in-a-lifetime opportunity to walk over hot coals and live to tell the tale, taught me that if I put my mind in the right state, I can accomplish anything.

We all need someone to provide us with reliable leadership and guidance. These people can provide invaluable support and perspective as you get your business up and running.

FOUNDATION #2:
ASSEMBLE A WINNING TEAM

As a franchise owner, you'll likely also be an employer, and the people you hire will help make or break your business. Your team will dictate the level of customer service you can provide, and they'll determine how confident and happy you can be about your operation when you're not personally on the job. If you're going to be operating on a semi-absentee basis—or if you intend to invest less of your own time in the long run—hiring the right people is doubly important.

As you set about staffing your franchise, put your full focus on bringing in the best people in the market—"A" Players—to help author your success. My good friend and executive business coach Rick Crossland has helped me—and in fact helps all his clients—to shape the culture of our organizations by hiring smart, dedicated, team-oriented employees. He recommends that we think of ourselves as talent scouts in this process—great advice. Rick defines A Players as the top 10 percent of talent available at a given compensation level. A Players are awesome, aligned employees, as opposed to B Players who are only average and C Players who are draining and detrimental. You deserve to have a team of 100 percent A Players.

Rick has generously given me permission to share his proven method for hiring A Player employees here:

Hiring Step 1: Define the Position.

Your first task in hiring is creating a positional agreement for each role. Rick calls these *A Player Agreements*. Think of this agreement as a job description on steroids. It should map out the major responsibilities of the job, and define the daily, weekly, and monthly activities needed to produce an A-level performance. It should lay out the critical drivers of success, key performance indicators, and the cultural values of your business. Use this document to make your expectations crystal clear to candidates. Positional agreements should be reviewed with the candidate and signed off by both employee and manager. The secret is in actively reviewing the contents of these agreements on an ongoing basis.

Many franchisors have already created positional agreements you can use for this step. If your franchisor has done so, take their experience to heart and commit to following those job specs to the letter.

Hiring Step 2: Market Like You Mean It.

Regardless of the state of the economy, author and *Fortune* columnist Verne Harnish is right when he says, "The war for talent is on." Whether you're looking for a CPA or someone to man a service counter on Friday afternoons, always assume you're in competition to hire the best employee for your business. To that end, your job posting needs to be compelling enough to excite your prospective employee with the match between the position and his or her aspirations.

Your posting also needs to get noticed. Online, refresh it on a daily basis so it stays near the top of all listings. Don't hesitate to spend money on your posting's placement just as you would on advertising and marketing. Bringing top candidates to your business will pay for itself in the long run.

Hiring Step 3: Build a Bigger Candidate Pool.

While you should always be looking for quality over quantity, creating a bigger candidate pool increases your odds of finding an A Player for your job opening. The number of candidates will be influenced by the position you're filling, offered compensation, required skill level, and geography. Within the limitations of those specifications, though, you want as many solid candidates as possible.

One key point in building a candidate pool is to not allow any candidates to backdoor the process. Business owners sometimes directly interview candidates referred by a friend or colleague or skip steps in their hiring process because they're in a hurry. Not only is this a recipe for potentially selecting a subpar candidate, but it can also damage personal and professional relationships if things don't work out. Always direct referrals to the entry point of your hiring process. Great candidates often come from referrals, but by putting them through your standard hiring process, you won't have to wonder if you've made the right choice.

Hiring Step 4: Use a Hiring Hotline.

Business owners often complain about the ineffectiveness of reading through stacks of resumes—and they're right. There is a better and more predictable way of reviewing candidates. Rather than spending your time on generic—and often padded—resumes, try setting up and automated hiring hotline.

The benefits of this approach are many. First, you can easily sort through hundreds of applicants for a single position by reviewing these three- to five-minute recorded files. Second, you'll get a sense not just of a candidate's job history, but also of demeanor and ability to think quickly in answering questions. Third, you'll get a relatively genuine and accurate snapshot of your applicants when they're answering your specific questions.

Hiring Step 5: Get the Group Together.

Once you narrow your candidate pool down to a dozen or fewer applicants, consider using a group interview to assess their skills and suitability for your position. On interview day, gather your top candidates, along with any trusted employees you've already chosen. If you are just beginning to staff up and don't have employees on board yet, choose two or three trusted colleagues or advisors to fill this role. Have each interviewer prepare a few questions that ask about their past performance.

Open the meeting with a short presentation about your business and the job's positional agreement. Let the candidates know they'll each get the same questions and that you'll rotate the order in which they receive and answer them. You'll be surprised at how much less repetition in answers you get by doing a group interview rather than individual ones. Candidates know they need to differentiate themselves, so they'll work harder to come up with original responses in a group. At the conclusion of your questions, ask candidates for their own questions.

An entire group interview typically lasts an hour or two—a huge time advantage for you over taking an hour to interview each person. Plus, you'll benefit from the input of the team members or advisors who go through the process with you. After the candidates leave, compare notes and select one or two finalists to come back for callback interviews.

Hiring Step 6: Conduct a Behavior-Based Interview.

A person's past performance is the best indicator of how he or she will perform in your company, so you want to ask questions designed to discover the facts of your candidate's experience. Behavioral-based questions seek detailed, factual answers and will give you far more useful responses than hypothetical or projection-based questions. Go through your candidate's prior positions job by job. Prepare a set of questions to repeat for each past position—questions that get at specific responsibilities and results. This should be an opportunity for a promising interviewee to shine.

Hiring Step 7: Interview References.

Many times, business people are so eager to extend an offer and hire a good candidate that they either rush through or are tempted to bypass reference checks. Treat these calls as a continuation of the interview process, not just a rubber-stamp check.

Just as your one-on-one interview with the candidate focused on past performance, so should your reference interview. Your franchisor may provide questions, but if not, be sure to ask previous employers about your candidate's job responsibilities, strengths, attitude, and whether he or she would be rehired.

Hiring Step 8: Perform Background Checks.

Almost there, but one final stop in the process! Use a reputable company to conduct a criminal background check. This process will not only check for criminal history, but can also serve to validate the applicant's educational and professional credentials. If your state laws allow, also run a credit check. It will provide a good indicator of your candidate's stewardship of money, and most candidates will either directly or indirectly come in contact with your company's revenue stream or expense structure.

At the end this last step in the hiring process, you should be able to feel very confident in offering your candidate a job!

One Caution

One important note to keep in mind as you begin hiring is that every employer needs to be familiar with the laws that protect against discrimination and invasion of privacy during the hiring process. This is an area where your franchisor will likely provide you with guidelines, but since you will be selecting your candidates and doing your interviews, you must take personal responsibility for understanding how the law pertains to employee selection.

FOUNDATION #3: LAUNCH WITH CONFIDENCE

When you're trained, staffed up and ready to go, it's time for your big launch. Your first one hundred days are critical, so leverage every available resource during this important time to ensure you're off to a fast start.

Roll Out the Red Carpet for Launch Pros

Many franchisors augment your headquarters training by sending out a launch advisor or team to work side by side with you in your first week or early weeks of business. The presence of one of these teams is an invaluable resource, not only to make sure you are get through your launch with flying colors, but also for your employees to get some expert hands-on help in adopting the franchisor's systems and working well within them.

If your franchisor does provide onsite coaching and support in your early days, make the most of it by addressing any questions or concerns you have right up front and face to face.

Follow the System

I know you've found this nugget of advice on many pages in this book, but it bears repeating, because in many ways, it is the key to franchising success. Every good franchisor (and what other kind would you partner with?) has invested a great deal of time, money, and experience in fine-tuning processes for everything from billing and bookkeeping to marketing and recruiting. The franchisor has tested and retested the products, supplies, and processes it shares with you—and every franchisee that came before you has tested them as well. The biggest favor you can do for yourself as you begin life as a franchisee is to think of *Follow the System* as your mantra for success.

If you run into trouble, get confused, or just need some guidance, turn to your franchisor and the process they have in place for answering your questions and offering support.

In the long run, you may very well come up with ideas for improving or fine-tuning your operation—maybe ideas worth taking back to your franchisor for consideration as part of its system. Smart, innovative franchisees come up with genius suggestions all the time, and many franchisors welcome those ideas and give them serious consideration.

While you get your feet wet and familiarize yourself with every aspect of your new business, though, stick with the programs that have been proven to work! Remember to master the system before you earn the right to innovate it!

Get to Know Fellow Franchisees

By investing a franchise, you have joined a marvelous peer group. It's very much to your advantage to develop relationships with other franchisees. They can give you great ideas and recommendations, and they can also share lessons they've learned the hard way to spare you some aggravation. A lot of new franchisees fail to leverage this valuable resource, but I strongly advise that you don't overlook it.

Some franchisees may have regularly scheduled get-togethers, while in other cases your franchisor might connect you with an existing franchisee who will serve in a "big brother" type role. In addition, don't forget the franchisees who were helpful to you during the validation process. They can be a great resource as you move forward and dig in to your business. These people are great sounding boards for you. Even if a spirit of competition exists among individuals, you and your fellow franchisees are teammates now, and you can look to the players who've been around longer to give you good advice about getting ahead.

Keep in mind as you utilize this incredibly valuable resource that it won't be long before you're the player who already knows the ropes and has valuable advice to offer—be sure to be responsive when your turn to be the "big brother" or sister comes around!

> *You and your fellow franchisees are teammates now, and you can look to the players who've been around longer to give you good advice about getting ahead.*

FOUNDATION #4:
MAXIMIZE YOUR MOMENTUM

Momentum is that elusive quantity that pushes a business from startup to success and from success to growth. I like to think of it in terms of a locomotive—a simple block of wood can stop a train with no momentum, but once that train gets moving along at full speed, not even a concrete wall can hold it back.

In business, momentum is achieved through the cooperation of a number of factors, and your franchisor will already have some of those in place. You'll be starting out rolling with a great concept, a streamlined process for delivering it, and a sophisticated marketing plan in place. But to really increase inertia for your business, you have to latch on to those advantages and push them forward with your own contributions.

Help bring your franchise to full speed by providing the unique skills and perspectives that only a business owner can implement with success:

Give Your Customers Winning Service.

The best possible endorsement of your business is a happy customer. We touched on customer service in theory in Chapter 2, but as your business picks up momentum, this becomes the elusive "It Factor" that can drive you forward or slow you down. Abraham Lincoln once said, "Whatever you are, be a good one"—better advice may never have been given. No matter what job you are doing in your new venture, do it to the best of your ability—and then follow it up with stellar, unimpeachable customer service. Your first customers—and all those who come after—should have a level of experience that they can share with colleagues, neighbors, and friends.

Customer service may be the most underrated factor in franchise success, but you can choose to be a business owner who knows better. One study estimates that 70 percent of buying experiences are based on how customers feel they're being treated. Another tells us that 55 percent of customers would pay extra to guarantee better service. And here's one more stunning stat: 96 percent of unhappy customers don't complain, but 91 percent of those will leave and never come back.

What is there to learn from statistics like these about customer service? Customer service is *not* primarily about how you handle complaints. It's about how you treat every person who walks in the door or gives you the opportunity to provide a service. As a new business owner, you will work incredibly hard to bring customers to your product or service. Once you've established a relationship with those customers, you must continually earn their business by providing a professional, polite, friendly, and overall outstanding experience. Consider these key factors in making that happen:

Attitude: Teach your employees to be cheerful, attentive, patient, responsive, and positive. Your franchisor's training program may help instruct workers in some of these attributes, but you can reinforce them every day by demonstrating them yourself.

Effectiveness: We've all had the experience of going into a business and being treated with great kindness—but little effectiveness.

Whether you're dealing with a waiter who can't keep an order straight, an accountant who overlooks an important tax deduction, or a well-meaning but incompetent sales person, nothing will lose your business more quickly than not having it done well. Give your employees the tools they need to work knowledgably and efficiently, and reward them for accomplishing those goals. Be prepared to handle not just the routine transactions, but the inevitable surprises as well.

Responsiveness: Actively seek feedback from your customers through the channels your franchisor provides—and take it to heart. Always strive to improve on the customer service experience you offer. Your willingness to listen, to cooperate, and to coach your employees to ever-better service will be a key factor in keeping your customers coming back time and again.

Be the Leader Your Business Needs.

Next to keeping your customers happy and coming back, the next big factor in business momentum is keeping your employees happy as well. Your capacity to motivate, lead, and support your employees will drive your business forward day after day and year after year.

In your experience as a parent, partner, or manager, you've likely already learned the lesson that, "Do as I say, not as I do," is a failing leadership strategy. If you want people to believe in you and look to you as a leader, you need to demonstrate the characteristics you value most. As an employer, you have the potential to influence the lives of the people who work for you for the better, and this is true whether you're hiring educated professionals, trade workers, or part time support staff. So be the person who embodies the values you believe in, and be the most proactive member of your team when problems arise.

Henry Ford once gave the wise advice, "Don't find fault. Find a remedy." As a business owner and as an employer, this is a bit of wisdom to take to heart.

Above all, remember that truly great leadership is the kind that makes your employees share your goals and believe in the success you are creating together. Connect with the people around you. Demonstrate your own commitment not just to the business, but also to the team members who will author its success.

Be Ready to Respond to Growth.

You went through all the steps to get your business off the ground, survived the startup, stabilized, and now you're seeing the fruits of your labors in the form of sustained momentum. Congratulations! Your business is moving full-steam ahead.

As you reach that great point of acceleration and accomplishment, be ready to make your next move. Whatever your business needs to grow, this is the time to make it happen. Whether you need to add a crew, expand your territory, build on strategic relationships, take on more accounts, or expand your services, don't be afraid to harness the momentum you've achieved to move forward. This is the moment when your vision and action can put you on a path to long-term, large-scale success.

SUCCESS STORY:
FINALLY HEARING THE INNER VOICE

Background: After twenty-five years in the telecommunications industry with responsibilities all over the world, Todd had survived several rounds of layoffs. When it finally happened to him, he was forty-eight—too young to retire but not interested in relocating to pursue a similar job.

Search Process: Todd and his wife had some savings to leverage and didn't want to move, so they met with me about the possibility of buying a local franchise that might eventually replace his corporate income. I suggested a number of possibilities for the couple to consider at our second meeting, and they were drawn to the business model of a kids' fitness program.

Decision: The couple invested in the martial arts for kids franchise.

Result: "I don't wake up in the morning wishing I had a hundred emails from people around the world with problems for me to solve," Todd says of his new life. "I don't miss wrestling with issues I can't resolve because half the people involved have just been laid off. You trade one set of concerns for another, but I am not for one moment longing for the life I knew before."

Best Advice: "If you're wondering if this is an option for you," Todd says, "I suggest you listen and discover if you have that little voice in your head saying, 'I'm not sure I can see myself doing this for another twenty years.' I had that voice in my head for a very long time. I only wish I had listened to it sooner."

CHAPTER SUMMARY

- The franchisor has a vested interest in your success, so every education and training program it offers has the potential to be instrumental to your business. Be sure to avail yourself of every opportunity.

- The franchisor has tested and retested the products, supplies and processes it shares with you—and every franchisee that came before you has tested them as well. The biggest favor you can do yourself as you begin life as a franchisee is to think of *Follow the System* as your mantra for success.

- Having "A" Player employees is critical to your success. Investing your time, energy and resources in choosing productive, positive employees will enable your business to work without you. Poor hiring choices can plague your business with ineptitude and poor customer service.

- In business, momentum is achieved through the cooperation of many factors, and your franchisor will start you rolling with a great concept, a streamlined process for delivering it, and a sophisticated marketing plan. To increase the inertia those components bring, augment them with your outstanding leadership, customer service, and vision for the future of your business.

THE NEXT STEP:

Go to the **HIRE YOURSELF** *resource page to learn more and take action*

WORKSHEET:
Finding Your "A" Players

WORKSHEET:
Making the Most of Your Proven System

Go To:
HIREYOURSELFBOOK.COM/Resources

ARE YOU READY TO HIRE YOURSELF?

"Control your own destiny or someone else will."

—JACK WELCH

hether you're currently employed but dissatisfied with your job, in career transition, or dreaming of owning a business, I hope this book has introduced you to a potentially rewarding next step in your professional development. I firmly believe that franchising is a viable, often better, alternative to traditional employment.

This book was designed to provide a foundation of knowledge about a potential career path that could positively impact every area of your life. My goal is to give you a dose of courage—and encouragement—to control your destiny. The days of a one-company career and paycheck security are nearly gone. Why wait for the ax to fall when you could start living life on your terms now?

You probably caught an underlying theme in the franchisee success profiles in the book; they all decided to take control of their lives by betting on themselves.

If I've piqued your interest, you owe it to yourself to explore further. Next, take these steps to determine whether or not franchise ownership is for you:

1. Align with your loved one on your dreams and goals. Make a commitment to keep an open mind and explore the path of franchise ownership.

2. Schedule a free consultation with a franchise consultant. This will give you a quick insight on the fit of franchise opportunities with your skill set, interest goals, and financial capability.

3. Leverage the information and recommendations in this book to investigate and invest in a franchise business.

I hope this book helps give you the confidence to write your own success story. If you are open to exploring the path of becoming an entrepreneur through franchise ownership, feel free to reach out to me for assistance with your journey.

Thank you for investing your valuable time in reading this, and I wish you much success in the future.

Thank you,

Pete Gilfillan

ACKNOWLEDGEMENTS

I would like to acknowledge my thanks to all the special people who've supported me in my journey to write this book. First and foremost, I thank my awesome family—Shannon, Alex, Sarah, Kate and Lauren—for believing in me and for sacrificing many family evenings and weekends so I could write.

Sincerest thanks to my mentor Darren Hardy, for making me want to try to make a positive difference in other people's lives, and for encouraging me to become an author.

Thank you to Rick Crossland, my business coach and good friend, who pushed and guided me to follow my dream of writing a book.

Thanks to Shelley Taylor, the talented writer who assisted with writing.

A very special thank you to Jana Murphy, the exceptional "Book Doctor" who helped me take the book to the next level.

Thank you to Jeff Elgin, FranChoice Founder/CEO and franchising industry expert, for his many reviews, critiques and suggestions that helped the book become a more valuable resource for readers.

To the candidates who've allowed me the privilege of guiding them through the process of franchise investment and helped me become ever more convinced that this is a legitimate and over-looked path to self-determination and personal wealth—I thank you for your trust and for sharing your success stories.

Lastly, thanks to all the folks at Advantage Media for their unwavering support in the editing and publishing of my book.

ABOUT THE AUTHOR

Pete Gilfillan is a passionate business leader who is driven to help people achieve their dreams of career independence through franchise ownership. With more than twenty years' experience as a corporate executive across multiple industries and a history of small business ownership, Pete brings a wide breadth of experience to his work as a franchise consultant. His unique knowledge of franchising, energetic outlook, and determination to find the right franchise for each candidate's lifestyle and goals set Pete apart in his field.

In some ways, Pete's been in franchising all his life. He was raised in an entrepreneurial family where both his father and grandfather owned successful franchise enterprises. As a young man, Pete spent seventeen years working at Ford Motor Company, rapidly advancing through a variety of regional and national positions to reach the role of general manager—where he guided up to six hundred franchise dealerships generating $5 billion in revenue. In his executive capacity, Pete was able to gain an in-depth knowledge of the mechanics, strengths, and benefits of franchising from the corporate side of the table.

Pete became a franchise owner himself in 2010 when he purchased a multi-state master license to a junk removal franchise. His investment gave him the opportunity to better understand the benefits and challenges of being a franchisee and the importance of choosing the right franchise for one's strengths, talents, and business objectives.

Since 2011, Pete has been working as an independent franchise consultant with FranChoice to help potential franchisees gather information, evaluate opportunities, and make smart selections in franchise ownership. In his role of helping each candidate find his or her optimum investment and lifestyle choice, Pete has found his most fulfilling and rewarding professional calling.

Pete is a graduate of the University of Wisconsin–Eau Claire and resides in Naperville, IL, with his wife and children. In his private life, he enjoys watching his kids' activities, spending time outdoors, exercising, and avidly pursuing self-improvement through books, audio programs, and seminars.

Pete@HIREYOURSELFBOOK.COM
855-904-7900
HIREYOURSELFBOOK.COM